# Rathlin's
## Rugged
### Story

*from an Islander's perspective*

*8 August 2005*

*by Augustine McCurdy*

*Augustine McCurdy*

Printed by
Impact Printing
Coleraine and Ballycastle

# ACKNOWLEDGEMENTS

I wish to thank all of the following individuals **and bodies for their help** and contributions in various specialist fields:

| | |
|---|---|
| Nikko Gruger and Angela | Research and loan of antiquarian books |
| Kathryn McFaul | Research and loan of documents |
| Loughie McQuilkin | Information on the Coastguard Service |
| Mrs Judy McCurdy | Drawings of kitchen and fishing boat |
| Neal McCurdy | Various drawings |
| Mrs Marie Feeney | Photographs of John Roe McCurdys |
| Mrs Dora McCurdy | Photographs of Gaelic League boats |
| Philip Cummings | Tapes of Isabella McKenna nee McCurdy |
| Gabrielle and her father | |
| Seamus McCurdy | Photographs of school children 1930 |
| Paul McCurdy | Geology of Rathlin |
| John W Arthurs | Geological maps and information |
| Rev. G. MacAteer | Irish language translations and songs |
| Dr Richard Warner, | |
| Ulster Museum | Provenancing of Rathlin Brooch |
| Dr Ian Meighan, | |
| Queen's University | Provenancing of porcellanite axes |
| Prof Michael Herity, | |
| UCD Dublin | Neolithic period |
| Commissioners of Irish Lights, | |
| Dublin | Rathlin Lighthouses |
| Northern Ireland | |
| Public Record Office | Various documents |
| Ulster Museum, Belfast | Photographs of Robert Welch and Alex Hogg |
| Linenhall Library, Belfast | Various documents |
| Belfast Central Library | Francis Joseph Bigger papers |

and last, but by no means least:

| | |
|---|---|
| Alison Hurst, Rathlin | Word-processing and deciphering my handwriting |
| Tommy McDonald of Impact Printing Ltd., Ballycastle | Technical help and proof-reading |

# PREFACE

My interest in history goes back to my childhood. My father had books on Irish history, some of them had references to Rathlin. I can recall spending many winter evenings, reading these by the light of an oil lamp or the fire.

It was many years later, when living away from Rathlin, that I began to understand what I had read. Since returning to Rathlin I have often been asked by visitors about the history of the island. It was these requests which eventually made me decide to set down a record of Rathlin from the point of view of an islander.

In the Twentieth century there have been great changes. I have seen a traditional lifestyle disappear. That lifestyle was one of self-sufficiency where a family lived off a small farm, the land was ploughed and crops sown each Spring and gathered in the Autumn. There is no longer any land cultivated, the only crop now is grass silage.

What I have written will help to answer visitors' queries. It will also serve as a reference in future years and will, I hope, give some flavour of life on the island over sixty years ago, as well as its earlier history.

Tomas O'Crohan, when writing of the Great Blasket island, in the early Nineteen Hundreds, said that, "The like of us will never be seen again." I think this could also be said of the old Rathlin people of the same period.

*A. D. McCurdy,*
*Garvagh*
*December, 1999*

# CONTENTS

# THE ORIGINS OF RATHLIN ISLAND

If there could be a single event or starting point, in the vastness of time, when Rathlin could be said to have first appeared in anything like its present form, that point would have to be around 60 million years ago. This was a time when dinosaurs were still on earth, although almost at the end of their reign.

The land that was to become Rathlin and Ireland lay far to the south of its present position, appearing where Morocco in north Africa is today. If that is so, how is it that we are now in the north Atlantic? The answer is continental drift. Geologists are now aware that the various land masses are not fixed forever in one spot, they are continuously on the move, floating on the molten core of the earth, as leaves float on water.

The land mass that comprised Europe and North America began to split apart 60 million years ago. North America, including Canada and Greenland, started to drift westwards and are still doing so today. The gap that opened up was soon filled with sea water, and so the Atlantic Ocean began as a strip of water, just a few miles wide. This split in the land mass was to have dramatic and long lasting consequences in the area that was to become Co. Antrim, Rathlin, western and lowland Scotland. As the continents drifted apart, the rock base was stretched and thinned, this caused weaknesses in the earth's crust, cracks appeared over large areas of the landscape which, at this time, consisted of shale or limestone covered in a variety of vegetation, mainly grassy plains. Molten lava welled up through these cracks and flowed out over the land, in a manner similar to the Icelandic lava flows of the present day. This process continued for some 2 million years and then became quiet.

The basalt rock thus formed began to weather and break down into a reddish fertile soil. This weathering continued for several million years. Vegetation, including trees, began to colonise the new land surface, in what was by then a warm and damp sub tropical climate. This development was interrupted by further outpourings of lava, which wiped out the vegetation and buried it under deep layers of basalt. This new basalt can be seen on Rathlin throughout Cleggan and Kinraver, in Ballyconagan and near Ushet Lough. This basalt makes an excellent building stone, as it splits fairly easily and gives a good face, which stonemasons have used for many generations on Rathlin. The soil and vegetation which was buried under these fresh flows of Tholeiitic basalt show up as red bands, several metres thick in places. It can be seen clearly in the north west cliffs of the island, near the lighthouse. Another more accessible site is alongside the road beside Ushet Lough in the townland of Roonivoolin. This second volcanic period came to an end around 50 million years ago. However, the land did not immediately settle down, there was widespread warping and cracking of the surface, which in turn caused considerable downfaulting throughout Co. Antrim and further afield.

**Causeway Type Basalt Columns at Doon Point, Rathlin**
**Photograph by Alex Hogg about 1915**

### Downfaults

Downfaulting is a geological term which describes the downward movement of large blocks of the earth, sometimes many square miles in extent. Rathlin is traversed by a number of deep faults which run in a north/south direction. These faults take the form of steep-sided valleys. One example of such a fault runs from Altachuile on the north coast through to the sea at Lacknakilly by the Church of St. Thomas. This fault reappears at Mill Bay and continues south east through Kinkeel, Ally Lough, Ushet Lough and into the sea at Ushet port. Another good example runs from Altandivan Bay on the north side, through Cleggan Lough to Oweyberne on the south side. The greatest of these downfaults in the north Antrim area occurs in the Tow valley at Ballycastle and runs in a north easterly direction past Rathlin towards the Mull of Kintyre. This fault caused a vast block of land to drop down some 200 metres and pulled the southern tip of Rathlin (Roonivoolin) downwards.

Another great natural force at work is erosion by the elements - wind and water, sunlight and frost. In the course of a lifetime, say 80 years, there are a number of rock falls from the cliffs, but they do not visibly alter the shape or area of the island. However, if we multiply this time by 1,000 or 10,000, very considerable changes will be evident.

## Ice Ages

A further force which shaped the landscape is the occurrence of the Ice Ages. It is uncertain when or why this process started, but it is known that at least 2 million years ago glaciers were advancing throughout the northern hemisphere. During this time the ice has advanced and retreated on a number of occasions. The most recent period of glaciation began to recede some 15,000 years ago and was finally gone by 10,000 years ago. When the ice flows were at their greatest, Rathlin was under an ice sheet upwards of one mile thick. The ice was continually on the move, and carried vast amounts of rock and gravel with it. The direction of travel of the glaciers can be seen in certain places, where the surface of the solid rock has been gouged out or striated. The ice carried rocks great distances. On Rathlin there are a number of 'erratics' in the Craigmacagan and Roonivoolin townlands. These are very large pieces of Scottish granite, they would probably be 2 or 3 tons in weight. The best known of these rocks are the 'Macatire' (The Two Wolves), two large lumps of granite leaning against each other in Craigmacagan. During this time the weight of ice pressed the land down by as much as 30 metres. When the ice started to melt, the sea levels began to rise fairly quickly. Beaches were formed from the vast amounts of gravel, sand and stones left by the melting glaciers. However as the ice receded, the land also began to rise as the great weight was removed. The geological term for this is Isostatic Uplift.

## Isostatic Uplift

This upward movement carried the recently formed beaches up out of reach of the sea and new beaches were formed. This has happened at least three times on Rathlin since the end of the Ice Age. The earliest or highest of these raised beaches is traceable in the townland of Roonivoolin. It is approximately 20 metres above the present sea level and would have been formed around 10,000 years ago. At this time Rathlin would have consisted of several rocky islets. In the townlands of Ballynoe, Demesne, Glebe and South Ballycarry there are large areas which are considerably less than 20 metres above present sea level and these areas would have been under water. The sea also ran through Crockascreidlin and Coolnagrock.

Between 8,000 and 7,500 years ago, as the land continued to rise, these areas would have begun to appear above water. Even at high tide, the limestone caves around the island, which were formed by the action of the sea, were now lifted well beyond the sea. The great bank of gravel which runs from the Manor House to the Rocket House and further to Mill Bay, was built up at this time by the prevailing westerly ocean roll, sweeping all the loose limestone along the south coast of Rathlin and piling it up into a raised beach which now forms the land of Glebe and Ouig, reaching its highest point (about 12 metres above sea level) between the Big Garden and the Rocket House. This beach extends all the way to Soerneog (kiln) in Kinkeel, although at this end, the limestone is replaced by basalt. This beach also occurs in the townland of Roonivoolin, extending from near the lighthouse, past Ushet port and on towards Doon point. This area has been cultivated in the past and forms a flat field, with a very steep seaward facing bank and, where rabbits have been burrowing, the sea-rolled pebbles can be seen, many of them are obviously carried from Scotland by glaciers.

The present day beaches, which are subject to the force of the sea, are also gradually being piled up and may also, in their turn, be lifted clear of the sea in 2,000 or 3,000 years time.

## THE FIRST INHABITANTS

### The First people

It seems likely that the first visitors to Rathlin would have been the Mesolithic people, who were hunters and gatherers of food supplies. They would have come from southern Europe, moving northwards as the ice caps and tundra conditions receded, at the end of the last Ice Age. At this period of time, 9,000 to 7,000 years ago, there would have been land bridges existing between Europe and the lands now known as Britain and Ireland. These land bridges allowed plants, trees, animals and insects and life of every kind to re-colonise these lands, which shortly before had been covered in glaciers, similar to the conditions now existing in places like Greenland or northern Scandinavia.

In the period of 1500/2000 years following the end of the Ice Age, trees of many types had moved in and developed dense forest, mainly broad-leaved trees, e.g. hazel, birch, ash and oak, rowan, elm and hawthorn. This was the landscape which the Mesolithic peoples first saw as they arrived in small groups. They were not farmers, but depended for food on what they could catch or gather, e.g. fish of all types, various game, such as deer or wild pig and various seeds and fruit in season.

The raw material which they needed for a limited range of tools existed in abundance in areas like the Antrim or Rathlin coastline. The limestone cliffs contain large amounts of good quality flint, which is easily knapped to make scrapers, knives, arrows, spear heads etc. These first settlers found everything they needed on the coastline and river estuaries. It is unlikely that they would have moved into the great forests, except on the occasional hunting expedition. It is worth noting that the climate through this period of time would have been warmer and drier. Researchers have estimated that the average temperature would have been 2 or 3 degrees higher than today, which would be similar to the northern coast of Spain at present, but with less rainfall.

## Second Wave of Settlers

The first inhabitants were followed by a more advanced people, known as Neolithic, or new stone age. Their arrival on Rathlin was approximately 5,000 years ago. At this time the land bridges across the Irish Sea and to Europe would have been submerged by the rising sea levels.

So how did they get here? Clearly they could build boats, some quite large. There is a dug-out boat constructed from a single oak log, over 50 feet long by $4\frac{1}{2}$ feet wide, in the national Museum in Dublin. This boat dates from the period of our Neolithic predecessors. Such a boat would be capable of crossing the sea, carrying possibly 10 to 15 people and some livestock. Maybe using the narrowest channels, e.g. Mull of Kintyre to the Antrim coast or Rathlin, or Galloway to Co. Down, or Brittany to Cornwall and Wicklow.

Where did they come from? It is likely that they came from the south eastern corner of Europe, around the Mediterranean, where they acquired a knowledge of farming. These people represent one of the great steps in the development of the human race. They were the first farmers. This knowledge of growing crops and keeping livestock allowed them to establish a settled pattern of lifestyle. They would not have travelled directly to Ireland. It is more likely that it was a slow migration westward, along the great river systems of Europe, the Danube and Rhine. This movement of people would have taken several generations, eventually arriving in Ireland.

Why did they come to Rathlin? The most likely explanation is that they were looking for suitable materials to make stone tools, axes, etc. Upon arrival on Rathlin they would have been confronted with a very different landscape from what it is today. Sea levels were much higher, somewhere in the region of 40 to 50 ft. above present levels, this can be seen from the raised beaches at Ushet an around the harbour area and also clearly seen at Kinkeel. The land around Ballynoe and Ouig would have been under water, the sea-rolled white gravel in the fields indicate this.

Where would the Neolithic people have beached their boats? The shortest sea crossing would be from Murlough bay to Ushet. It is likely this is the route they used. Their first visits would have been by way of exploration, possibly no more than a day trip. Their boats would have been very similar to the currachs still in use on the west coast of Ireland. They would have been up to 30 feet long and lightly built. It would be quite feasible to undertake such a trip today in a skin-covered boat from Murlough, landing at Ushet on a summer's day and walking around and exploring at least the lower end of the island.

## Rathlin's Forests

Movement on foot would not have been as easy as it is today. Land which is now cultivated would have been covered in fairly substantial forest. The sides of the hills, where the land is poorer, would have been covered in hazel and possibly juniper. Heather may have existed on the hill tops, although the climate at this stage would not have encouraged its growth. The trees at this time would have been oak, elder, ash or birch, mainly growing on the good land.

## Buried Trees

We know that Rathlin was well forested in the Neolithic period. Evidence for this lies in the tree trunks and branches uncovered during the cutting of peat and various deep drains. When my father was cutting peat in the 1930s, in a small peat bog near the cliffs at Garvagh, after draining the bog which required a drain about 8 feet deep, the top foot or so was soft brown turf and then about 5 or 6 feet of hard black turf. At the bottom of this were large quantities of hazel branches, trunks and layers of hazel nuts up to 6 inches thick. Some layers of nuts were broken up into tiny fragments, in other layers the nuts were mostly whole. Below the peat the base was very hard, compacted grey brown earth, not clay. This would indicate that when these hazel trees were growing, perhaps 3 to 5 thousand years ago, the climate was very different from today.

Rainfall must have been very low. The hollow which held the peat would not have been filled with water as it is now. If we follow this through, the areas of bogland which now exist elsewhere on the island would have been dry land for most of the year in the Neolithic period. In other bogs, where turf has been cut, and also in the draining of these bogs, fairly large tree trunks have been uncovered. The large trees obviously grew on the deepest soil, hazel, mountain ash etc. would have been growing on the sides of the hills and generally on lighter soil.

## Brockley Axes

We do not know how long the Neolithic people had been visiting Rathlin before they found the outcrop of porcellanite at Brockley. However, having found it, they would quickly have established a settlement. Porcellanite rock was the best material around for the manufacture of axes and other tools. This isolated outcrop represented power and wealth to those in control of it. They had a rare material that was in great demand.

We can see the scale of working from the vast spoil heap of waste material which lies at the base of the rock face, probably in the region of several hundred thousand tons. The method of quarrying the rock was likely to have been by lighting fires to heat it up, and then quenching it with cold water. This method is still used to break up large rocks. There was no shortage of wood for fires as they would have been systematically clearing trees from the land to grow crops, barley, wheat and a few other plants. Originally their settlements were around the edges of the woods. Chipping floors i.e. where the axes were manufactured, have been found on a number of sites within a mile of Brockley. These are in places where the soil was too poor to grow crops.

## Dwelling Sites

There are a number of stone foundations throughout the island which are the remains of Neolithic dwellings. They are mostly on high ground, where no-one today would consider building a house. This is a further indicator that the climate then was much milder than the present.

## Pottery and Axes

There have been a number of finds of artefacts, pottery and polished stone axes etc., dating from the Neolithic period. Among these recorded are pottery

**Porcellanite Stone Axe with wood haft**

and a polished stone axe fragments uncovered on a Neolithic dwelling site near Ushet Lough in the townland of Roonivoolin, by Mr Hewson. These items are in the National Museum in Dublin. Other pottery fragments were found in Ballinagard by Mr Whelan in the 1930s. More recently, the Ulster Museum have carried out excavations on a site in Knockans townland. The pottery etc. uncovered is still being cleaned and dated.

In addition to these sites, large numbers of porcellanite and flint tools have been collected in the fields during ploughing, the majority in the townlands of Ballygill North, Middle and South and Knockans, roughly within a mile or so of the source. These areas would have been fairly well forested and settlement was around the edges of the forest initially. The numbers found would indicate that they were discarded as they became blunted, either in felling trees or cultivating the soil. Most of the axes found were roughly chipped to a cutting edge. These would have been adequate for field work. The polished axes found are small in number and were probably only used on ceremonial occasions. The immense effort needed to polish them would not have been justified merely to use them for felling trees or cultivating fields.

## Cultivation Methods

The method of cultivation would have been quite different from anything we visualise today. To prepare a field for planting grain, they would have burnt off any weeds then, at planting time, using a stone axe with wood handle fixed to it, a small hole was made and several barley or wheat seeds dropped in. Using this method a field could·have been planted by a family in a few days. The disadvantage of this simple method is that, after a few years of single cropping without use of fertiliser or ploughing, the soil would become depleted of trace elements and minerals and so the crops would decline, thus forcing a move to fresh ground and further tree clearance!

## Stone Circles and Burial Mounds

Apart from dwelling sites, there is other evidence of continuous occupation of Rathlin. There are still existing several stone circles, one or two cairns and at least one burial mound, also remains of an ancient field system and several other enclosures, possibly fields. There were, in Knockans townland at Shandragh, two stone piles, possibly burial mounds. The stones from these were used for road building around two hundred years ago. These, together with other structures, have vanished and were incorporated into the stone wall field boundaries which were also built during the 18th and 19th centuries.

## Lifestyle

Having established that the people of the Stone Age (Neolithic) lived on Rathlin, perhaps we can try to visualise the lifestyle of a typical family group. A family would have included relatives of two or three generations, living and working together for the common good.

What sort of houses did they live in? We know from archaeological research in other areas of Ireland that houses were both circular and rectangular. Foundations still existing on Rathlin are of the circular or oval type, from 15 to 20 feet in diameter. These stones were the foundations, the house would have been constructed of timber poles for walls and roof. Walls would then be laced together in the manner of a wicker basket, then plastered

**A Neolithic Dwelling**

inside and out with clay or mud. The roof would be thatched with whatever was available - barley or wheat, straw or reeds, or rushes. The floor was clay worked smooth by hand and, when set, covered with rushes.

## Cooking Methods

Cooking or bread making was done outside of the dwelling at a specially built hearth site. Water was boiled in a stone lined pit, by means of putting heated stones into the pit full of water. Meat or fish were cooked in this manner, bread was baked on heated stones. So we build up the picture. Our Neolithic family would have kept goats, sheep and pigs. There was also plenty of fish and shell fish and wild birds. Salt was collected from rock pools on the shore. They were self sufficient on Rathlin.

During this time there would have been regular contact with other groups in Ireland and Scotland. Some of these groups would have visited in the course of trading for porcellanite axes, other groups may have had more aggressive intentions, that is, the take over of the rock source. No doubt there were some fierce battles on Rathlin. This more or less settled way of life continued for at least 1500 years without any major changes.

### New Immigrants

About this time a new group of immigrants appeared on the scene. These people we classify as Bronze Age. They would also have come from Europe. No doubt there was confrontation between them and the old Neolithic stock.However, these new arrivals brought new skills - both in farming and metal working skills. They had the ability to use copper and tin, to make a range of copper and bronze tools. This represented a serious threat to the ancient trade of porcellanite working and a loss of income and status to the Neolithic people, no doubt they resisted these newcomers initially. However, as we know, progress of the human race is irresistible.

We do not know for certain whether bronze tools were actually manufactured on Rathlin, there are no known deposits of copper or tin ores. However, copper ore did exist, close at hand, in the Antrim mountains. There is a scarcity of artefacts on Rathlin which could be attributed to the Bronze Age period. There are, however, a number of graves near to the present harbour, which have been dated to this period. This district is called Ouig, which translates to 'tomb' or 'grave' in Irish and Scots Gaelic. Whether these Bronze Age burials are all of Rathlin natives, we do not know. Some may have been brought to Rathlin for burial. There is an old story that the Bronze Age people always buried their dead across water. This was to ensure that their spirits could not return to annoy them. It is now unlikely that we will ever know the truth of this.

There appear to be two separate burial grounds in this area. The second one is of the early Christian period and is situated in the field with the old name of 'Parc na Chloch Bhiorach' (The field of the pointed stone) i.e. The Standing Stone. This burial ground is likely to have been in use during the existence of the Monastery founded by St. Comgall of Bangor, on or near the site where St. Thomas's Church now stands. In Christian burial sites, generally the graves are aligned east to west.

### The Celts

To return to the pre-Christian period, around 600 BC, another wave of Europeans arrived in Ireland. These were the Celts. At this period of history they controlled Europe from the Black Sea to the Atlantic coast. Their main power base was the area now forming southern Germany, northern France, Switzerland and northern Italy. They had developed a materially sophisticated lifestyle and traded with the Greeks and other peoples of the eastern Mediterranean. They brought to Ireland considerable skills in working with iron and precious metals, particularly gold, which was then fairly easily obtained in Ireland. Possibly this wealth was what attracted them to Ireland initially. This time marked a considerable change in farming methods. The Celts preference was cattle grazing and not so much arable farming. Cattle represented wealth.Each animal had a price and could be traded for other merchandise. The downside of this system was that cattle were easily stolen and this happened frequently, perhaps the best known example of this is told in the great epic story ' The Tain', the cattle raid on the Cooley peninsula in the north of County Louth.

**Crannnog Lake dwelling as it might have looked at Ushet Lough, Rathlin**

Very briefly - there existed a brown bull in the Cooley mountains. He was generally the finest bull in all of Ireland. Queen Maeve of Connacht decided she must have this bull. At first, she tried to bargain for him. When this failed she assembled her armies to take him by force. Eventually she did succeed, but at a great cost to herself and Connacht. The warriors of Ulster were beset with a sickness and were unable to defend themselves. This is where the mighty warrior Cuchulainn, who was not from Ulster, came on the scene. Single-handed, he defended the interests of the Ulster kings, until they and their warriors began to recover from their sickness.

The cause of this inability to defend themselves has been the subject of debate in various learned circles, even in the Rathlin Bar. It is generally asserted that one of the oldest human failings, jealousy, was the cause of the sickness. They could not agree who would lead them in battle, as this would require acknowledging one leader above all others. This failing is still with us.

This is a story which is essential reading for anyone who wishes to get an understanding of early Celtic society, history and legends which existed in the oral tradition, many centuries before it was written down.

Essentially, the arrival of the Celts marks the transformation from the archaic peoples over a period of perhaps 1,000 years or so, to the beginnings of the early Christian period. They brought a culture and language which has lasted to the present day.

## Language of the Celts

Although early accounts of them paint a picture of a fierce, proud and warlike people, I think it can be assumed that the earlier Bronze Age races continued to survive alongside the newcomers, probably as a subject race. Eventually they would have intermarried and so the ancient blood lines would have survived into the present.

**The Rathlin brooch now in National Museum, Dublin**

Language scholars tell us that there are a number of words in the Gaelic which can be traced back to a pre-Celtic origin.

To return to Rathlin, there have not been many known finds of artefacts which could be dated to this early Celtic- Iron Age period. Of those which were found, some have disappeared, probably to private collections. Perhaps the best known of these is the Rathlin Brooch which is in the National Museum in Dublin. This brooch was uncovered in a grave, marked by Standing Stone, about the year 1780. It is made from solid silver and is of Celtic design and workmanship and appears to date from about 850/900 AD . The date is well outside our early Celtic period, however, in terms of design, it fits into that tradition of skill.

## Celts on Rathlin

The only structure which has been associated with the Iron Age period is Doonmore in Ballygill North. This is a natural circular hill, about 50 feet high, arising out of more or less flat ground. It has a flat top and is about 50 yards in diameter. There is evidence that the top and sides have been artificially shaped. There are traces of a rampart around the edge which is up to 12 feet wide and, within this, a rectangular building once existed, about 40 feet by 10 feet. Clearly, this was a substantial fort in its time. There are remains of a further fort on the cliff edge, some hundreds of yards north of Doonmore, and what appears to have been a stone causeway connecting the two. There are no records of any artefacts, other than a few stone axes, from this site. These two forts would have provided

**Quern Stone for grinding grain**

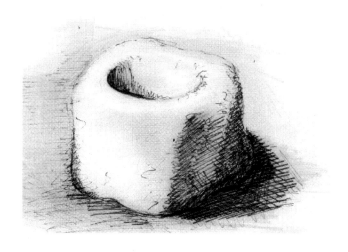

**Bullaun Stone for grinding grain**

an excellent view of the seas on both sides of Rathlin and any sea-borne marauders would soon have been spotted. It is likely that the small port of Dun na nGiall would have been in use at this time and later.

There may have been other coastal fortresses on Rathlin.There is mention in the old records of a fort at Doon on the east side of the island, although no trace of it now exists. It is possible that the site of Bruce's Castle was also fortified a thousand years before the castle was built. There are no signs of Raths on the island, and so our evidence of Celtic habitation is fairly limited. It is interesting that these forts were on the north and east sides of Rathlin, which face Scotland, the most likely source of raiding parties of Picts who then inhabited Scotland. Apart from raiding from both sides, there obviously was a considerable amount of trading with Scotland and Wales in particular.

## Celts and Romans

In the First century AD the Romans were in control of England, most of Wales and the southern half of Scotland. This presented opportunities for considerable trade for the Celts. The Roman Tacitus, writing in the First century AD, said that although the interior of Ireland was unknown, there was a better knowledge of its harbours through trade and merchants. The main exports were cattle, hides and wolfhounds.

The Celts or Scotti (as the Romans knew them) were establishing a foothold in areas of western Scotland such as Bute, Arran, Kintyre and Islay. This settlement appears to have started in the Third century AD, led by a minor Irish chieftain, by the name of Reuda of the Dal Reti, who settled with his followers in the islands of Arran and Bute. This was the beginning of the overseas expansion of the tribe of Dal Reti, who occupied the north eastern part of the present County Antrim, from the River Bush to Ravel Water, including Rathlin. As time went on, further expansion took place into the mainland of Scotland.This colonising must have been fairly peaceable, as we find that a hundred years or so later, in 360 AD, the Irish had joined forces with the Picts, to attack the northern frontiers of the Romans in Scotland.

## Fergus Mor

A further century or so later, about 470/480 AD, Fergus Mor and his brothers, Loarn and Oengus, led a party of 150 warriors from Murlough in Co. Antrim to Kintyre, in order to expand the territory of the Dal Reti and stamp their authority on this colony in the west of Scotland. Oengus settled in Islay, Loarn settled in the north of Argyll, near Oban, the district still bears his name. Fergus established the overlordship of the whole of these territories with a stronghold and royal residence at Dunadd, by Crinan Lough. Access was via the Crinan river from the sea. Fergus was installed as the first king of the Dal Reti in Scotland.

## The Stone Of Destiny

In order to perform this ceremony in the traditional manner, Fergus was given the use of the Stone of Destiny (Lia Fail) by his Uncle Murtagh Mac Erc, who was High King of Ireland at this time. The Stone was carried from Tara to Dunadd via Rathlin. We are not told who carried out the coronation ceremony, however, it is likely that it was none other than Murtagh Mac Erc, as we know from later times that the new kingdom was subject to the overlordship of the High Kings of Ireland. This eventually led to a dispute which involved Columcille in the following century. Scottish Kings lists are traced from Fergus and the Stone of Destiny was always used at their coronation ceremonies until it was taken from the Scots by Edward I of England in 1297. The Stone was subsequently installed under the coronation chair in Westminster Abbey in London, where it remained (apart from a short disappearance in the 1950's) until 1997, when it was returned to Scottish stewardship. It now rests in Edinburgh. According to tradition, this Stone was brought to Ireland by the early Celts and so its origins go back into pre-written history. It may be as old as the history of the Celts, over three thousand years.

## Early Christians and Saint Patrick

We now enter the early Christian period. St. Patrick, who started his mission in Ireland in 432 AD, in his lifetime established churches in many places. The townland of Kilpatrick in Rathlin seems to indicate that he, or one of his disciples, may have spent time on the island. It is said that Fergus Mor and his brothers had accepted the Christian teachings of Patrick, before leaving Ireland. This extension of the Dal Reti kingdom into Scotland was destined to have far reaching consequences over the ensuing centuries for Scotland, England and western Europe, both in political and ecclesiastical matters.An ancient tradition says that the whole of the kingdom of the Dal Reti could be seen from the peaks of Arran.

## Columcille

Columcille was the next major figure to arrive in the newly established territory of the Dal Reti in the year 563 AD. He was born in Donegal in 521 AD. His father was Fedilmith of the northern O'Neills who held High Kingship for many centuries. His mother was Ethne, from a Leinster tribe, subject to the southern O'Neill. As a youth, Columcille went into training for a religious life and adopted the Latin name Columba for monastic use. When he had completed his training, he founded a monastery at Derry in the year 545 AD. In the year 561 AD there was a battle took place at Cuil Dreimne in Sligo, between the northern and southern O'Neill. Columcille seems to have been held partly responsible for this. Be that as it may, two years later, in 563 AD, he sailed from Derry with twelve disciples. According to some reports, his immediate family also went with him. This journey follows the coast, via Rathlin, to Kintyre. Tradition says that he landed at Keil Point from where he went forthwith to see Conall at Dunadd, who was at this time king of the Dal Reti.

## Conall, King of the Dal Reti

Columcille was not arriving among complete strangers. He was distantly related to Conall and, after he had given an account of the battle of Cuil Dreimne to Conall and who the victors were, Columcille was given the island of Iona by Conall, where he proceeded to found a monastery.

In the years to follow, Iona was to become the centre from which the Christian teaching was spread throughout Scotland and northern England and further afield into Europe.

## Aggression from Co. Down

Columcille was called upon at times to resolve territorial disputes between rival kingdoms. One such occasion arose when a tribe, known as the Dal nAridi, whose territory extended from Larne through much of Co. Down, including Bangor, decided to attempt to annexe the lands of the Dal Reti in Co. Antrim. If they had succeeded, they would also have gained control of the Scottish kingdom which, of course, was still at this stage under the ultimate control of the O'Neill.

At this time Aiden was king of the Dal Reti. He did not relish the idea of submitting to another tribe, however powerful they were. He was fortunate in having Columcille present in his territory, as through him the link with the O'Neill was maintained.

In the year 575 AD a council was called at Druim-Cete which has been identified as being at Mullagh, not far from Limavady. Those who attended included Columcille, Comgall of Bangor, Aiden, king of the Dal Reti and Aiden of the O'Neill. The main outcome of this council was the strengthening of the alliance between the O'Neill and the Dal Reti, thereby excluding the Dal nAridi from gaining any foothold in Scotland. Columcille made a number of trips to Ireland, usually following the coastline via Rathlin. At least one of these journeys lasted several months when he founded the monastery of Durrow in County Offaly about the year 585 AD. Throughout Columcille's lifetime and the centuries following, Rathlin or Rechru, as it was written in the old Irish, is often mentioned.

In Adomnan's Life of Columba, there are several events mentioned, as follows:

Colman was sailing to Scotland when he ran into bad weather in the whirlpool of Brecain. This is called Sloc-na-Mara, and in the ebb tide off the Rue Point on Rathlin, with a north west storm blowing, forms a fierce sea with overfalls which can cause trouble to large ships. Anyhow, Colman resorted to prayer and eventually made it to Scotland. The whirlpool of Brecain is a historical reference to the disaster which befell Brecain and his fifty currachs in the year 440 AD when on a trading mission to Scotland. They encountered the seas of Sloc-na-Mara, with the total loss of all hands. On another occasion, when Columcille was a guest in Rathlin, a man called Lugne Tudicla, who was a pilot "probably guiding ships around Sloc-na-Mara, as well as into ports on Rathlin", came to him and told him that he and his wife could not get on together. She had an aversion to him. However, Columcille persuaded them to pray and fast with him over a day and a night. On the following day the problem was resolved and, in the words of Adomnan, "let us pass on, from that day, until the day of her death, that wife's affections were indissolubly set in love of her husband".

### Lugaid of Iona

Columcille, whilst being a respected figure within the Church, was obviously a skilled diplomat. Whether in individual disputes or arguments between rival kingdoms, he carried immense influence in Scottish matters. During Columcille's lifetime, there was a monk by the name of Lugaid, who acted as emissary on many journeys to Ireland, on the instructions of Columcille. He is credited with having founded a monastery on Rathlin.

### First Church on Rathlin

It is said in "The Life of St. Comgall of Bangor" that Comgall made two attempts to found a Church or Monastery on Rathlin. The story told, of his first visit to Rathlin and being forced to leave by thirty armed men, could be explained by the fact that he was outside of his territory. Rathlin was inhabited by the Dal Reti, who were loyal to their kingdom and also to Columcille and, by extension, to the O'Neill. Comgall was from Bangor in the territory of the Dal nAridi, who in turn, were subject to the Ulidians, who were often at odds with the O'Neill.

I have mentioned earlier the Council of Druim Cete, following which, when Columcille and Comgall were resting at Dun Cetheru (now known as Sconce Hill, west of Coleraine) Columcille refers to this difference in their origins. It is said that Comgall succeeded in establishing a monastery on his second visit, about 580 AD. If he did, it was likely by the leave of Columcille, as the rule of Columcille extended throughout both parts of the Dal Reti, including Rathlin. It is worth noting that in the period from about 550 AD to 650 AD, monasteries were proliferating at a great rate. Throughout Scotland the larger monasteries were acquiring numbers of lesser foundations, which laid claim to being established by the Mother Church, or had affiliated themselves to the latter. This served two purposes; it allowed territorial expansion on the one hand, whilst remaining within the protection of the main establishments, who usually enjoyed good relations with the provincial kings. Columcille died on 9th June 597 AD.

## Segene, Abbot of Iona

In the year 635, Segene, who was Abbot of Iona, founded a Church on Rathlin. At this period it was not difficult to found a monastery. It only required two people of religious mind. They did not have to be ordained. Rules for founding a Church were more stringent. Cummene was the seventh Abbot of Iona, after Columcille. In the year 661, he came to Ireland. At this time there had been some serious breaches of undertakings made to Columcille many years earlier.

## Cummene of Iona

Cummene spent some time in the territory of the Dal Reti, including Rathlin Church. He resolved the problems and wrote about this whilst in Rathlin. This indicates that Rathlin was within the rule of Iona. This situation continued without any serious problems until the year 790 AD, when Iona and Rathlin suffered the first Viking raids.

## Viking Raids

Iona was again attacked in 802 AD, and in 806 AD sixty-eight persons of the settlement were killed by the Vikings. In the year 807 AD the Iona community began to build a new settlement at Kells in Co. Meath and moved there shortly afterwards. It was during this century that Rathlin came under the rule of Bangor. The Vikings made further raids on Rathlin in 973 AD and 1045 AD. In the raid of 973 AD, they pillaged and destroyed what they could not remove. They also put Feredach the Abbot to the sword, and no doubt others, whose names were not recorded.

The last recorded raid associated with the Vikings occurred in 1045 AD, when they killed 300 including the chieftain Randal O Heochada.This period of Viking raiding and settlement brought great changes in the kingdom of the Dal Reti, or Scotti, as they were also known. They formed alliances with the Picts of north and east Scotland, under a common royal dynasty. They then annexed the kingdom of Strathclyde and the lowlands, and drove its royal elite into exile in Wales. These events brought about the end of the ancient united kingdom of the Dal Reti. From this time on the Dal Reti of Antrim and Rathlin were on their own, although contact was maintained with Scotland.

## Monastic Sites on Rathlin

There exist on Rathlin at least four sites which have had monastic settlements in the past. Three of these most likely date from the early Christian period, before the Viking raids. They are Cill Bhride in Ballygill townland, Cill na Bhruain in the townland of Knockans (Cill naoimh Ruain), Cill na Bhruain in the townland of Carrivindoon. The fourth is in Kilpatrick, where the circular stone foundations of monastic cells still exist. These sites are in addition to the site where St. Thomas's Church now stands. This was the principal monastic settlement in early Christian times.

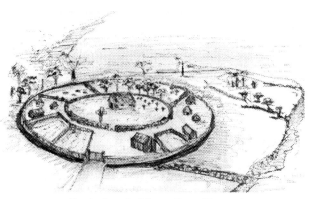

**Typical early Monastic settlement**

**Monk's Seat, Knockans**

## The First Norman Invasion

Rathlin does not get a mention between the massacre of 1045 AD and 1213 AD. By this time, the Norman invaders had succeeded in taking control of England, Wales, Ireland and most of Scotland. The first of these Normans in Antrim was John De Courcy. He had been granted, in 1177, by Henry II, as much land in the Ulster province, as he could take by the sword and hold. He was successful in this, as within three years, by 1180, he was one of the largest land holders in Ireland. The castle on Rathlin is supposed to have been built by him.

The castle at Carrickfergus was built by him as his principal fortification. As in all dealings of men, success breeds jealousy in others. This was certainly the case with De Courcy. He was soon removed from his holdings and replaced by another Norman, Hugh De Lacy, in 1205. De Lacy did not last long, as by 1210 AD he was hunted to Scotland by King John. In the year 1213 AD Rathlin was included in a grant of lands to the earl of Galloway.

By the year 1242 AD Rathlin again changed hands. This time the new owners were John and Walter Bysett who, having been accused of murder in Scotland, were told to leave and never return. They promised to go to the Holy Lands and take part in the Crusades. However, Co. Antrim and Rathlin were much easier to get to. Throughout this period of history, it appears that the way to obtain a large land holding was to accuse the existing holder of treachery and yourself to swear unflinching loyalty. Rathlin appears to have suffered another massacre around 1274 AD.

## Robert The Bruce

The next major event on Rathlin was the arrival of Robert Bruce, King of Scotland. Bruce had been crowned King of Scotland in the Abbey of Scone on 25th March, 1306. This event was not to the liking of Edward I of England and so he set about raising an army to invade Scotland and have himself installed as King. Bruce did not have the resources to stop this assault and was forced into a retreat. A number of disasters befell Bruce. He clearly had decided, some time before, that he would make for Kintyre, where he had a staunch friend in Angus Og McDonnell of the Kingdom of the Isles. It was in this direction he headed. He and his small band crossed Loch Lomond in an old boat they found sunken in the reeds. It could only carry three at a time. From here, they made their way, with the help of the Earl of Lennox, to the Firth of Clyde, where they obtained galleys to take them to Kintyre. Their first landfall was at Sandell Castle which was under the control of Angus Og McDonnell, then at Dunavertii on Kintyre, which overlooks Sanda Island. Upon hearing that he was still being pursued, Bruce, with the help of Angus Og, moved to Rathlin in November 1306 AD. Rathlin was a safe haven, as the Mc Donnells and allied clans controlled the seas between western Scotland and the coast of Antrim. Bruce also had some relations and influential friends in Ulster.

## The Spider

Bruce arrived in Rathlin in November 1306 AD with a small band of supporters. These included his brother-in-law, Sir Neil Campbell, and Sir James Douglas, known as 'Black Douglas', a fierce warrior who was Bruce's right hand man. It was during this stay on Rathlin that Bruce is said to have gained inspiration from a spider. He was certainly in need of inspiration at this time as he had lost everything he ever had - his family were imprisoned by Edward I and his lands at Carrick in Ayrshire, confiscated and redistributed. Bruce watched the spider make six attempts to swing across a gap in the rocks, to put the first thread of its web in place. On the seventh attempt it met with success. Bruce said to his men, "If this small creature has the tenacity to keep trying until it succeeds, then so can I."

## Highlands and Islands

During the next two months he set about gathering support in the western Islands and Highlands with the help of Christiana of Mar, a relation, by marriage, and heiress to considerable lands. He returned to Rathlin in mid January, with a fleet of galleys and many clansmen. A few days later Sir James Douglas set out with a small party for the Isle of Arran. Under cover of darkness and with the element of surprise, they took Brodick Castle, which held a considerable quantity of supplies and arms. Ten days later Bruce joined them with 33 galleys. Shortly afterwards they made a landing on the coast of Ayr, near Turnberry Castle. Rathlin's role ends here, but, as history tells us, Bruce went on to fight a guerrilla war and eventually regain the Kingship of Scotland at the Battle of Bannockburn on June 24th, 1314. It had taken almost eight years, but the inspiration from the spider on Rathlin had stood him in good stead.

Incidentally, there are other caves in Scotland called after Bruce, but I think this can be explained by the type of guerrilla campaign which he carried on. He and his men lived in forests and caves throughout those years. He did not feel safe in a castle or any building constructed by man. After the visit of Bruce, there were no major events recorded on Rathlin for over two hundred years.

## MacDonnell and Bisset

One matter worth mentioning was the marriage of John Mor MacDonnell to Margery Bissett in 1399. This John Mor was the grandson of Angus Og who had helped Bruce. Margery Bisset was the heiress to considerable lands in Co. Antrim, including Rathlin. She was descended from John Bysset, one of the brothers who had been banished from Scotland in 1242 AD.

Rathlin's next involvement in serious trouble happened in 1551 AD. By this time the MacDonnells had become powerful landowners in Antrim. They had come into conflict with the O'Neills on several occasions. However, the event which triggered off Rathlin's involvement was a raid which the MacDonnells made on the lands of the O'Neills in south Antrim, then known as Clandeboye, and carried off great spoils, which they secured on Rathlin. These spoils included cattle and horses. An account of the succeeding events comes in a letter from Thomas Cusake, (the then Lord Chancellor in Dublin) to the Earl of Warwick. Cusake organised a military expedition to Rathlin to wreak havoc on MacDonnells. This expedition consisted of three hundred soldiers, gunners and archers under the command of Bagnall and Cuffe.

## Invasion Turns to Disaster

Upon arrival at Rathlin in barques, they only had enough boats to land about one hundred men. Their plan was to capture MacDonnell galleys which they could see drawn up on the beach. To this end, they attempted to land with four boats, each carrying about 30 men. This was accompanied by volleys of shot from the barques. The first boat contained Cuffe and Bagnall and twenty-eight soldiers. While they were attempting to land, a heavy swell put their boat on the rocks. The waiting MacDonnells immediately attacked them and killed all except Bagnall and Cuffe, whom they took prisoner. The attack on Rathlin finished in disaster for the Crown forces, as, according to another report, many more were killed by the MacDonnells.

The two prisoners were exchanged for Sorley Boy MacDonnell who was being held in Dublin at the time. To get their own back, the survivors of the Crown forces landed at Ballycastle and went to Kenbane Castle, which belonged to the MacDonnells and knocked down some of the walls, it must have been unoccupied at the time, as the letters make no mention of anyone being killed. In the year 1557, Rathlin was again attacked by Sir Henry Sidney, who claimed to have slaughtered every living thing.

## Difficult to Live on Rathlin

Throughout this period and indeed for the following century, it would have been very difficult, or maybe impossible, for anyone to have led a normal life on Rathlin. It was used by the MacDonnells as a base for their various operations in Co. Antrim, and was in turn attacked for this reason. Over the next few years Rathlin remained fairly quiet, until July 1569 AD. There now occurred an event which was completely different from anything that had gone before. This was the wedding of Turlough O'Neill, chieftain of his clan, to Lady Agnes Campbell, widow of James MacDonnell. This marriage had more to do with political alliance than anything else. Lady Campbell was able to bring three thousand Scottish redshanks, the fierce Highland and Isles mercenary soldiers, to augment the O'Neill and MacDonnell forces in their continuing campaign against the Crown forces.

It is said that at this time Sorley Boy McDonnell built a house on Rathlin for the newly-weds, with the finest orchards in Ireland This is likely to have been Ballynoe house, which, apart from the castle, is the oldest building on Rathlin. The McDonnells still retained ownership of this house and forty five acres around it in 1861.

Rathlin did not long enjoy this peaceful state. In July 1575 an invasion took place on the instructions of the Earl of Essex. This was under the command of John Norris, assisted by Francis Drake. The castle was the first place attacked, with the use of heavy canon landed at Port a Mhuillin. All who had taken refuge there were killed, with the exception of the constable and his family, who were taken prisoner and released a month later. This was his recompense for surrendering the lives of all within the castle. When this deed was completed the Crown forces were ordered to sweep the island and kill everyone they could find. Many had hidden in caves, but they were smoked out and slaughtered.

According to tradition there was only one survivor, that was a woman called McCurdy, who had managed to escape the massacre, probably concealed in one of the more inaccessible caves. Many of those killed were soldiers of the MacDonnells. Six weeks later Sorley Boy McDonnell returned the compliment. He led an assault on Carrickfergus Castle and killed over one hundred of the soldiers who had taken part in the massacre on Rathlin.

### Uninhabited Island

The island appears to have remained uninhabited after this event for some years, although there were some McDonnell clansmen present from time to time. One of these occasions was in March 1585, when the island came under attack by the Crown forces led by Sir Henry Bagenal and Sir William Stanley. According to a John Price, writing to Walsingham, Chief Secretary to the Queen, "the island of Rathlin is very barren, full of heaths and rocks and there are not any woods in it at all." This is hardly surprising, considering that it had been the scene of various battles and a massacre in the preceding two decades. It was also uninhabited at this time, so clearly no crops were grown and there was no livestock.

There were a couple of incidents happened at Ballycastle in January, 1584, which are worth recording. In a letter written by Stanley on 5th January, 1584, he had marched to Ballycastle with a company of foot soldiers and horse. The horses were stabled in Bonamargy Abbey. At eleven o'clock at night a company of Scots arrived and created havoc among the Crown forces, including setting fire to the Abbey roof and burning the horses stabled there. Stanley came out in his shirt. He was wounded several times with arrows and as he says, "Of these wounds I am very sore."

### Scot's War Galleys

The next day, to add to his problems, there was sighted 24 Scottish galleys, rowing from Kintyre to Red Bay. He estimated that they carried 2500 armed men. Stanley's ships in Ballycastle Bay could do nothing about this as they were becalmed. I suspect they chose not to tangle with such a powerful force. These Hebridean galleys were lightly built long boats with a single mast and square sail amidships, with 20 oars, ten aside. They could move at great speed, carrying 100 men and land in any creek or beach. It is recorded that a McDonnell from Kintyre landed 900 men on Rathlin in three hours. Modern motor boats or ferries could not do any better.

### Trying to Land Supplies on Ballycastle Beach

To return to Stanley in Ballycastle, luck was not with him. A storm blew up and his ships could not land supplies. In the end, they used rafts on long ropes, with men wading into the sea up to their necks, on 20th January. He says that much of the supplies were lost, and no doubt a number of his men. Any man who stands on Ballycastle beach today in mid January with a nor-west gale blowing can well imagine the problems he faced. After these events, Rathlin was fairly quiet for the next half century or so. In 1615, Sir James McDonnell was brought to Rathlin for safety from Kintyre, when he was under pressure from the Campbells.

In the year 1605, Randal McDonnell was given a grant of the seven territories of the Glyns and Rathlin. In 1617, a legal dispute arose about the ownership of Rathlin, a George Crawford claimed that an ancestor of his had been granted Rathlin by James II of Scotland in 1500. Considerable evidence was brought by both parties to support their cases. In the end the decision went in favour of Randal McDonnell, on the grounds that there were no snakes on Rathlin and so it must be part of Ireland, as snakes exist in Scotland.

### No Snakes on Rathlin

An interesting piece of evidence was used in this case. Giraldus the Monk, who came to Ireland in 1170, said that in the old writings, snakes had been brought to Ireland in brazen pots, but on coming within sight of the land of Ireland, they died and so to this day, Ireland and Rathlin are still free of snakes.

During the sixteen hundreds, the plantation of Ulster was proceeding. Great tracts of land were confiscated from the native Irish and re-distributed to settlers from England and Scotland. This policy eventually led to the great rebellion of 1641. Many thousands were killed throughout Ireland in this period, but nowhere suffered more than Rathlin.

Charles I, King of England, had made an agreement with the Scots to send an army to Ireland to help put down the rebellion. The Marquis of Argyle got a commission making him temporary Governor of Rathlin, the island being used as a base for the troops supplied by him for the invasion of Ireland. Under the terms of this commission Argyle was given authority to expel or exterminate any rebels he might find there. In 1642 Argyle sent to Rathlin 1600 soldiers, under the command of his cousin, Duncan Campbell. There were, in Rathlin, a number of McDonnells as well as a small resident population. What followed was, in a large part, a vendetta between the Campbells and McDonnells.

### Invasion and Massacre by the Campbells

The battle took place at Lag-an Bhriste Mhoir, "The Hollow of the Great Defeat" This is in Glebe townland. There is a hill to the east of this field called

Cnoc na Scrioidlaine: "The Hill of the Screaming". It is said that the women stood on this hill watching the battle taking place in the field below, and were screaming. No doubt urging their men on, but also bewailing the slaughter taking place. The islanders stood no chance against this army, who were driven by hatred both religious and clan.

Having finished with the men, they then drove the women and children over the cliffs at a place since called 'Sloc na cailleach', "The Chasm of the Women".

"The island was swept bare of any living thing."

### Hearth Tax Rolls

After this disaster, Rathlin was again uninhabited for a time. However, in 1669, twenty seven years after the Campbell massacre, we have the first list of the names of people living on Rathlin. In 1662 the Government had introduced the Hearth Tax. This tax, which was at the rate of two shillings (10p) on every hearth, was paid by everyone except a few very poor people. The Hearth Tax Roll of 1669 for Rathlin contains the following names in each townland:

| | |
|---|---|
| Kinramer | Brian McCurdy, Pat McVicar, George Mc Gregor, Alex. McCurdy, Turlough O'Caine. |
| Ballygill | Arch. McGreige, Neile McCaffrey, Neile McCally, John McMulrogh, Thomas McMulrogh, Robert Allen, Pat Black |
| Kilpatrick | John McAllister, Widdy McAllister, Malcolm McKinley, Neile McQuaid, Art. Black. |
| Ballynavargan | Pat McHarge, Daniel McCormack, Wm. McComment, Finlay McColt, Finlay McCormack. |
| Ballycarry | Malcolm McQuonne, Donell McDonald, Augustine McCow, Andrew Boyd. |

These twenty six names represent the householders liable for this tax. If we assume that each house had at least three occupants, and also allowing for a few who did not have to pay, it would appear that the population was in the region of eighty or ninety people. There is no other reliable census of the period.

The earliest reference which I have discovered to the seven townlands of Rathlin is in the Inquisition at Carrickfergus on 3rd January 1603. These are listed as Kinkeel, Ballynoe, Ballynavargan, Kilpatrick, Ballygill, Kenramer and the half townland of Ballycarry. It was stated that Queen Elizabeth seized possession of the island in 1585, together with everything in it, including a ruined castle and it seems that these townlands existed at this date. The reference to the half townland of Ballycarry brings us closer to the point when Ballynoe was created by the McDonnells, as this townland was previously part of Ballycarry. It is also stated that the island is worth £5 sterling per annum after all deductions. Presumably this is the rent collected by the McDonnells, as it is also stated that the tithes belong to the Abbey of Bangor.

In William Petty's survey of the McDonnell lands there are seven townlands listed on Rathlin. These were very much larger than they are today and covered the whole island. It is noticeable that in the Hearth Tax rolls, only five of these townlands are listed as being occupied. These are all on the high ground, well away from where the massacres had taken place, or where invaders could easily make a landing. The two townlands not occupied are Ballynoe (Baile Nua) and Kinkeel (Ceann Caol), both on low ground. Six of these townlands were known from early times. The seventh, Ballynoe, was created by the McDonnell's prior to 1569 and included the present two townlands of Glebe and Demesne, as well as part of Ballycarry. It is generally agreed amongst Gaelic scholars that the great majority of place names on Rathlin are Irish in origin. A number of these place names also occur in the west of Scotland and the islands. This is not surprising, as the Irish language was taken to Scotland in the early Christian period.

## The Naming of Places in the Gaelic System

When we look at these townland names individually and take into account the Gaelic system for naming places and setting boundaries, we begin to get a clearer picture of how and when Rathlin placenames came into existence. The Gaelic system used the physical shape of the land to describe it and name it. This is a system that comes from the oral tradition, long before writing was invented. Another instance of where this tradition is preserved is in traditional songs in the Irish language. The old style (Sean Nos) song where a journey is undertaken, names every place which the traveller or the poet (na fili) journeys through. In this way names are remembered and passed on to succeeding generations.

The origin of the name of Rathlin goes back well before recorded history. Some scholars suggest that it may be pre-Celtic. The first reference to the island in a Gaelic form which I have come across is in Adomnan's "Life of Columba of Iona." These are Rechrea and Rechru. It is tempting to try to make a connection between Rechru and the Dal Reti, who were the inhabitants from pre Christian times, however, if we stay with the Gaelic system of using the physical features for placenames, then a visitor approaching Rathlin would be struck by the rocky appearance, not only of the cliffs, but of the landscape. Upon landing on the island and travelling across it, it presents a series of rugged and rocky hills. I believe this physical appearance is the key to the meaning of the name. In all the numerous translations and frequent mis-spellings which I have come across, I think that John O'Donovan, in the Ordnance Survey of 1827, may have come closest with "rocky island", although it is difficult reconcile the Gaelic word for island "Oilean" with this. ·

Returning to the seven townlands listed by Petty, of these 'Kinramer' (Ceann Reamhar) the thick or broad end, and 'Kinkeel' (Ceann Caol) the thin or narrow end, describe the island exactly and are therefore the oldest, possibly dating from the early Christian period. The third townland name, not now in use, Ballynavaragan (Baile na Faireacan) which means the ledged or terraced land, again describes this area exactly. This old townland included the present townlands of Ballyconagan, Church Quarter, Mullindreas, Ballynagard, Glebe and Demesne. The eastern boundary followed the natural fault line, which is the present boundary with Ballycarry. The western boundary followed the natural fault, north to south, which forms the present boundary between Ballynagard and Kilpatrick and South Knockans.

## The Townland of the Cauldron

The townland of Ballycarry (Baile an Choire) the townland of the Cauldron. This word Choire occurs in several placenames on Rathlin and in each case refers to a place where a stream tumbles over or through rocks and gives the appearance of boiling as a pot or cauldron. In the case of Ballycarry, this boiling effect happens in the boundary stream and also in the sea offshore from the East Lighthouse, where the tides meet. These four townlands take their names from the natural physical features. Of the remaining three townlands, two take their names from historical events and the third from the actions of the then owners, the McDonnells.

Ballygill (Sean Baile Ghaill) the 'Old Town of the foreigner or lowlander'. This name Sean Baile 'Old Town' occurs in various places throughout Ireland and usually refers to a deserted dwelling site, sometimes deserted for many centuries. Ballygill may have been given this name by people who saw the ruins and, not knowing who they were, called them strangers. These foundations are of an earlier time than the 17th century. Additionally, the ruins of Dunmore would have been much more visible 400 years ago than at present. Also parts of the ancient field system in North Ballygill have survived until the present. The workings of Brockley porcellanite would also have been very evident. It is likely that the name Ballygill has arisen from all these signs of human activity, stretching back over 6,000 years.

According to folklore, all the people of the upper end of the island once lived in Ballygill. This refers to the area around Ballygill hill, where, apart from existing buildings, there are remains of old foundations right around the hill.

The years between 1586-1641 were a relatively quiet period, Rathlin and the Glynns were under the control of the McDonnells. Rathlin was re-settled during this time.

## Kilpatrick and The Franciscans

The townland of Kilpatrick (Gila Farik) the 'Church of St. Patrick', is associated with religious worship from early Christian times and indeed there are relics of pre-Christian usage from the neolithic period. Its position of dominance overlooking most of the island, and with views of both Ireland and

Scotland, make it an attractive site. Tradition says that St. Patrick visited Rathlin and preached from the hill Cnoc Patrick. This may have some truth, as he was closely connected with Armoy, which is not far away on the mainland. Islands held an attraction for religious people, where they could get away from the world and develop their spiritual life.

In more recent times, there was a monastic settlement of Franciscans in Kilpatrick. This was close to the south eastern boundary, adjacent to the small, hidden field of Achadh Beg (small field), or, as it is sometimes called, Altbeg (small height). This field and the altar stone (Cloch an Aifrinn) were the site of the principal mass station on Rathlin during the period when the penal laws were in force. There is a look-out stone nearby. This field overlooks the site of the Franciscan establishment. Some of the circular foundations of the monastic cells still exist. Most of the stones were used in the building of Kilpatrick wall in the 1850s. When the Third Order of Franciscans were driven from Bonamargy Abbey, by Crown forces, they set up a refuge in Glenshesk, near Ballycastle and later in Rathlin at Kilpatrick.

The first mention of a priest on Rathlin is Friar Dominic Brallaghan (Bradley) in the 1730s, he was of the Franciscan Order.

**Baptismal Font**

Amongst the items which the Friars rescued from Bonamargy was a baptismal font. This font was eventually installed in the first Catholic Church built in Ballycastle. When the present Church was built, the old Francisican font was donated to the Rathlin Catholic Church, where it did service for many decades. It eventually started to leak and so it was put outside. The last time that I saw this ancient artefact was near the former priest's house, where it was being used to grow flowers.

The boundary wall around Kilpatrick was built in the 1850s and 60s. It is known as the Famine Wall. All the men in the Upper End of the island worked on it. They were paid two shillings and sixpence per week, (i.e. 12p). Kilpatrick was used for grazing a herd of Highland cattle. The building which housed these animals still exist. The original Kilpatrick included Knockans, again the boundary with Ballygill followed the natural physical features of the land.

**New Town**

The townland of Ballynoe (Baile Nua) new town, was created by the McDonnells around the end of the 16th century. It incorporated the southern ends of Ballycarry and Ballynavaragan and included the present townlands of Glebe and Demesne. It provided a suitable setting for Ballynoe House, which was a substantial, well built and finished dwelling, constructed for the use of the McDonnells of Antrim during their various sojourns on Rathlin.

In the year 1746, the Revd. John Gage of Aghadowey, near Coleraine, purchased a long lease of Rathlin from the McDonnells. The price paid was £1,750. The McDonnells retained fishing rights and some mineral rights, as well as Ballynoe House and 45 acres of land around it, the store at Ushet port and a house and nine acres of land in Church Quarter. This was still the case in 1861.

Revd. Gage did not live on Rathlin. However, when he visited he stayed in Ballynoe House until his death in 1763. He was succeeded by his son Robert, who also stayed in Ballynoe House before he commenced building the Manor House and living full time on Rathlin. Since that time, Ballynoe House has been put to various uses, apart from a dwelling. It was used as a Post Office and also as a Police Station. It is now used as a barn. Some of the ornate plasterwork still remains.

These are the seven old townlands.

## Sub-division after 1760

The island was further sub-divided in the 1760's, resulting in twenty-one townlands. Glebe was not separated until 1825, making the present twenty-two. The purpose of this sub-division was to facilitate the collection of the Grand Jury 'Cess' or Assessment Tax. The old townland of Ballygill was divided into North, South and Middle Ballygill. Kebble was walled from Kinramer. This wall enclosed the best grazing land at the west end of the island and was used by the Landlord for sheep, although tenants remained there until 1830. The meaning of the name has been translated from Scottish Gaelic as "The Family Memorial or Burial Ground." However, whilst it is known that a few burials did take place, there are other townlands which would have equal or better claim to this placename on the grounds of well known cemeteries. There is another translation which is more likely to be the correct one and this arises from the building of the wall to enclose the ground.

AnCaibeal equals 'the enclosure'. There is another district, in Ballynoe townland, called AnCaibeal. This also was an enclosure.

Cleggan (Cloigeann) RVB 1772, 'the Skull' This name describes the townland. There are a number of areas of bare rock visible as in bare skull, the bare bones of the land.

Knockans (An Cnocan) 'Small Hills' again is descriptive of this townland. RVB 1770

Ballynagard (Baile na gCeard) 'the townland of the tradesmen' e.g. smiths or metal workers. RVB 1787

## Ballyconagan (Baile Coinneagain) RVB 1780

It is said, on the island, that this name means the townland of the rabbits. However, Rev. William Hamilton, on his visit to Rathlin in 1784, says that there are no rabbits on the island and that Mr Gage had just recently introduced a few brace of hares. Mrs. Gage in 1850 says there are no rabbits present. So this townland name must have another origin. J O'Donovan, in the Ordnance Survey Name books of 1827 gives the translation as O'Conigan's town. This seems to be the most likely meaning. The surnames of O'Cuinneagain and MacCuinneagain are ancient Gaelic names which are widespread in Ireland, although in many different guises. Cunningham and Kinaghan are but two examples. There is a possible connection with Conaig, Son of Conghul, buried at Clonmacnoise.

I have been unable to discover a direct derivation of this name on Rathlin although in 1669 the name McQuonne is listed in the adjoining townland of Ballycarry. This name could be a derivation or even mis-spelling of McCuinneagain. In those turbulent times there were good reasons for adopting a different spelling of one's surname.

The townland of Church Quarter needs no explanation, other than to say that it designates the most ancient ecclesiastical district of Rathlin, which of course, it still remains.

The townland of Demesne means land directly attached to a mansion and not sub-let. This land was farmed directly by the Gage family and the name first occurs in 1788 in the Rathlin Vestry Book.

Glebe is the land attached to the Church for the Clergyman's benefit. In 1838 this land was 24 acres, 1 rood and 22 perches in extent.

Mullindreas (maoil na nDreas) is a direct translation from Maoil - Rounded Hill, Dreas - Briars or Thorns. This precisely describes this townland today.

Craigmacagan is another townland derived from a surname - Creag is Rock. Mhic Again or McAgan may be derived from O'Hagan, although again, there is no record of this surname on Rathlin. There are a number of fields, rocks etc. on the island named after individuals, though in most cases, Christian name only.

Carravindoon (Ceathru an Duin) the Quarter of the Fort. There was an ancient fort in this townland although there is now little evidence of its existence. The first reference to the name is in the Rathlin Vestry Book of 1775.

Carravinally (Ceathru an Eala). In the Rathlin Vestry Book this townland is listed, in 1772 and 1773, as Ally and in 1776, on the Maritime Map, as Carrivanhala and in the Ordnance Survey of 1827, as Carrivanally. Various suggested translations are the 'quarter of the pillar stone', 'quarter of the sanctuary'. However, the most likely is the 'Quarter of the Swan.' The word 'Eala' occurs in both Irish and Scots Gaelic with the same meaning, 'Swan'. These birds are still common visitors to Ally and Ushet loughs in this townland.

Roonivoolin (Rubha na bhFaoileann) is the southernmost townland of Rathlin and the closest to the mainland. It is first listed in the Rathlin Vestry Book of 1770. The word Ruba or Rubha occurs in Irish and translates as Point or Peninsula. Faoileann is seagull (Velan). So Roonivoolin is the point or peninsula of the seagull, and this is an apt description. Perhaps a more accurate spelling in English would be Roonavelan. On various maps of Rathlin this headland is written as Rue Point. This effectively translates as Point Point. This is one illustration of the kind of trap which we can fall into when mixing the Irish and English languages.

Apart from townland names, there are many other placenames on the island, running into hundreds. Some have been lost. To anyone who wishes to get a grasp of the extent and meaning of these names, I would recommend reading the Bulletin of the Ulster Place-Name Society Volume IV, which contains about 450 names with translations. Most of these names were supplied by Alex Morrison, native of Rathlin, to Donall MacGiolla Easpaig of the Placenames Office, Ordnance Survey, Dublin. It is a very valuable record of names which would otherwise eventually be lost forever. They remind us of a time when a different and ancient language was spoken on Rathlin. They also convey a more personal relationship with the land. The character of each field was often contained in the name, whether it was stony or rough or wet or sloping or clay etc. Fields and cliffs etc. were referred to by name.

Rathlin is a very rugged and scenic island. A walk along the road from Cnoc an Tairbh (Hill of the Bull) the westernmost point, to Rubha na Faoileann (Point of the Seagulls) the southernmost point, a distance of about seven and a half miles, will take the walker through fourteen of the twenty-two townlands as well as many other local field or place names adjoining the road.

## Population over the Centuries

It is likely that Rathlin has had a resident population since the time of the Neolithic people, although in that prehistoric period the numbers would have been small. It has been estimated that the whole population of Ireland at this period would not have exceeded 20,000.

The first time in history, when we can get a good idea of the population, is in 1669, as previously mentioned. The numbers would not have exceeded 100. In the succeeding one hundred years the population increased to almost 1200. There were several reasons for this dramatic increase. One was the increase in the population of Ireland during the same period from an estimated 1,100,000 in 1670 to around 4 million in 1780 and further to over 8 million in 1841.

Many who settled in Rathlin were refugees from persecution by Landlords and the Church, both in Ireland and western Scotland.

## Jacobites Forced Out

Following the defeat of the Jacobites in Scotland in 1689, those who had supported this cause were no longer welcome, particularly if they were Catholic.

At the same period the Highland Clearances were going on, when the Landowners decided that the four-footed tenants, i.e. sheep, were more profitable than the two-footed tenant. Many thousands were driven out of the Highlands and took refuge in the remote Scottish islands and Ulster, particularly in the Glens of Antrim and Rathlin.

Most of the Glens of Antrim, including Rathlin, were in the ownership of the McDonnells, who were powerful and influential Catholic Landlords of the old Gaelic stock and these refugee Highlanders were traditionally allied to the McDonnells of the Isles. Consequently, they felt they might have a better future in the Glens and Rathlin.

### Refugees after 1690

It was estimated by Archbishop Synge, in 1720, that 50,000 Scots settled in Ulster during the previous forty or so years. Many of these newcomers were soon to find disillusionment, as events in Ireland after 1690 created conditions whereby thousands of native Irish, as well as Scots, were displaced from their lands and sought refuge in the remote areas including Rathlin. The Penal Laws were enforced rigorously and those who were not of the Established Church suffered greatly. The Catholics and Scottish Presbyterians were persecuted in equal measure.

It was in the early years of the new century, i.e. 1700 onwards, that the great exodus to the New World began. The majority of these emigrants were Presbyterians, although many were Catholic, and became known in America as Scotch-Irish. These emigrants were later to play a decisive role in the American revolution.

The population of Rathlin increased considerably during this time. The next reliable figure we have comes from Bishop Hutchinson, who was Church of Ireland Bishop in the Diocese of Down and Connor, from January 17th, 1721. In that year he issued an appeal for help to build a Church on Rathlin, stating that there was a population of 490 people on the island who spoke Irish, and that they had neither Minister nor Priest settled among them. This figure of 490 represents an increase of around 400 in the 52 years since 1669.

The next substantial influx of refugees took place in 1745, following the defeat of Charles Edward Stewart, "Bonnie Prince Charlie" at the Battle of Culloden. Those who escaped took refuge where they could, many headed for Hebridean islands and also Rathlin.

There is an old story that these supporters, among whom were McCurdys and Blacks, smuggled Bonnie Prince Charlie to Rathlin, and from there he was taken to Lough Swilly in Donegal, where he had friends who organised his escape to France, although Scottish history says that after wandering for five months among the islands of the Outer Hebrides. He sailed aboard a French ship for Roscoff in Brittany on 20th September, 1746.

In the year 1766, the Bishop presented a report to the House of Lords, stating that the population of Rathlin consisted of 95 Catholic families and 26 Protestant families. The names are as follows:

Catholic: McCurdy (35); Black (14); McGillchrist (6); Morrison (6); McQuilkin (6); Anderson (6); McFaul (4); Millar (3); McCargy (3); McGowan (2); Roy (1); Rankin (1); McCay (1); Brallachan (1); McKermud (1); McKinley (1); McCurry (1); Walsh (1); McGregor (1); McKernan (1).

Protestant: McQuaig (6); Weir (4); McQuilken (4); McArthur (2); Walker (1); McAhergy (1); McKey (1); McCausland (1); Heraghan (1); McCully (1); Hunter (1); Dugal (1); McKinley (1); Rankin (1).

These 126 families would probably represent about 650 people.

In July, 1784, the Rev. William Hamilton visited Rathlin and, in his letters, states that the population was about 1200. He says that the Priest of the island held a census for the purpose of laying a tax of one shilling on everyone over the age of sixteen. This was intended to build a Mass House. From this census it appears that the population was 1100. Presumably this would refer only to the number of Catholics. This proposal was not well received by the people. They felt that such a tax would bring a death in each family so numbered. If only we could get out of paying taxes today on such a pretext! However, this proposal seems to have fallen through. If all these figures are somewhere near accurate, this represents an increase in population of around 700 in 65 years since 1721, a dramatic increase for a small island.

During the period 1720 to 1740, Alexander Stewart of Ballintoy was land agent for the McDonnells of Antrim, who were owners of Rathlin. The rent at this time was £109.7 shillings. The duties payable in addition to the rent were as follows:

| | |
|---|---|
| Kenramer : | 24 pullets and 10 sheep |
| Ballygill: | 24 pullets and 10 sheep |
| Kilpatrick: | 12 pullets and 5 sheep |
| Ballynavargan: | 24 pullets and 3 sheep |
| Ballycarry: | 12 pullets and 5 sheep |
| Ballynoe: | 24 pullets and 10 sheep |
| Kinkeel: | 24 pullets and 8 wethers |

The system of land tenure was fairly complicated, as there was much sub-letting of lands, e.g. the McDonnells leased the land to Alexander Stewart. This included Rathlin as well as a number of other estates on the mainland. This first lease was known as the chief rent. Stewart, in his turn, let out the land on short leases to a number of tenants, who were responsible for paying the rent set by Stewart, also the duties. These tenants, in turn, let the land by the year to others, known as cottiers. Profit was made from leasing except by the cottiers who were the last in line. This was the system on Rathlin.The townlands then existing were let to tenants of Stewart, these tenants sub-let the land to anyone they chose. It was in this way that many of the new immigrants found a foothold. They were coming to a place where they had connections, either clan or family. This applied particularly to the McCurdys and Blacks and explains the large numbers of each name. The new arrivals were coming among their own, whose connection with Rathlin is traceable back to 1300. In Michael J Murphy's book, there is reference to a story told by Mickey Joe Anderson of Glacanacre, relating how his grandfather had told him of the island being in four divisions at one time, with a head over each. These people were the chief tenants to Stewart and they would sub-let the land to their own connections.

## Start of Decline

The population of Rathlin remained at a high level until 1810, when the figure was 1150. From this point on, co-inciding with the end of the Napoleonic War, there began a steady trickle of emigration, some to Scotland and a few to America.

The only information on names of those emigrating directly from Rathlin to America is as follows:

Brig "Barkley", from Derry, arrived in New York 1816, John Black listed.

Ship "Westpoint" from Belfast, arrived in New York, November 22nd 1815, Archibald Black, John McCurdy, Neil McCurdy listed.

Ship "Alexandria" from Derry, arrived in New York, June 12th 1811, Daniel McFaul listed.

In the year 1813, the population was 1148 and in 1821 had dropped, by 68, to 1080, with a further drop of 70, by 1841, to 1010.

Dr. J D Marshall visited Rathlin in 1834 and spent some time on the island. In his fairly extensive notes, published by the Royal Irish Academy in 1837, he states that a great number of the young men go to Glasgow and Greenock, or to some of the ports in Ireland, to learn different trades, particularly that of ships' carpenters. He also says that, in recent years, a number have gone to America. In one of the years preceding his visit, upwards of forty had left for America and during the summer of 1834 sixteen had emigrated, so emigration was happening before the famine years of the 1840's. He says that the population was 1050 in the year of his visit, consisting of 900 Roman Catholics and 150 Church of Ireland.

By 1851 numbers had dropped by 257 to 753 and, by 1861, by another 300 to 453. Thereafter the decline was less dramatic.

Fifty years on, in 1911, the population was 351. However, the decline has continued until the present day. In 1937, a year I can remember, the population was 245, fifty years on, 1987, the numbers were 115. Ten years later, in 1997, the resident population during the week is 72. A few come back at weekends, bringing the numbers up to 82.

Rathlin's population has now reached the lowest point since the 1650s. A demographic study, carried out by J H Elwood, of Tory and Rathlin Islands, and published in 1971, covers the period 1841-1964. In his conclusions, he predicted that both islands would lose all of their populations and, in the case of Rathlin, this could occur by the end of this century.

Although this dire prediction will not happen by the end of the century (this is October 1998), things do not look promising. It is very unlikely that Rathlin will ever become totally depopulated, however, there are threats on the horizon. There is the possibility that if numbers drop considerably from the present, that services could be lost e.g. the school and the ferry service.

Another threat is that property speculators would move in and build numbers of holiday houses, which would only be used for a limited period during the summer and remain empty for the rest of the year. I have seen this type of development take place elsewhere. It contributes nothing to the local economy and would increase vehicular traffic considerably, on a very limited roadspace. It would make no contribution to the culture of the island which, despite the drop in population is still very much alive.

### Economy of Rathlin over the Centuries

Throughout the past centuries, the economy was based largely on self-sufficiency, with any surplus being sold outside to cover the rents etc. The main export, over at least two centuries, was a crop that did not have to be planted, but required a great deal of hard work to harvest. This was the seaweed which grew in profusion around the shores and still does to this day, although it is no longer harvested on Rathlin. According to Dr Marshall, the main seaweeds gathered were bladderwrack and tangles. These were cut at low tide and gathered ashore to be spread out in the sun to dry. In the evening it was gathered into small heaps like hay and next day, spread again. Around the shores of Rathlin it is still possible to see the remains of many small stone walls, built to spread the seaweed on for drying.

When a sufficient quantity was gathered and dried, burning would begin. This was done in a kiln, which was excavated near the beach. It was about five or six feet long, about three feet wide and two deep. It was lined with stones off the beach. A number of these kilns still exist. A small fire was started in the kiln, using dried heather or straw. The seaweed was then gradually added until it eventually became a red hot molten mass. Burning often continued, without a break, over a day and a night, being continually stirred with an iron rod. Upon completion of burning, the kelp was allowed to cool into a solid mass. It was then broken up and eventually boated to the kelp store, owned by the Landlord, where it was weighed and entered in a book. Once or twice a year a ship would call to collect it, most often from Glasgow, although it is recorded as being sold to the linen bleachers of Co. Antrim.

Chemical extracts from kelp were used in a number of industries. The main extracts were soda salts, potash salts, iodides, bromides and common salt. One of the principal products manufactured was iodine, which was used as an antiseptic. Extracts were also used in photography and dyeing of fabrics. It was used in glassmaking and soap-making and during the Napoleonic wars was used in the manufacture of gunpowder. I have been told that extracts of seaweed are currently used in the perfume industry and also as an agent for settling vats of beer. Potash, of course, was and still is, used in farming as a fertiliser. It is particularly good for potatoes.

According to an old record, 20 tons of seaweed will make one ton of kelp, from which 8 lbs of iodine can be extracted. Over the centuries the price of kelp varied considerably, often dictated by international events.

During the Napoleonic war, up to 1812, records tell us that the price of kelp rose to £20 per ton, and that 100 tons a year was being exported, to a value of £2,000. After the war ended, the price fell to £2 or £3 per ton. Dr Marshall, writing in 1834, says that only 30 tons were being exported. Kelp continued to be an important item in the island economy right up until the mid 1920's, when it finally ceased to be made. In the First World War, it again had reached a price of £20 to £40 per ton. In 1920 it fell to £16 and by the mid 1920's had fallen to £5 per ton. And so ended a long tradition of kelp burning. Modern methods of processing have made the old ways obsolete.

Other important exports were barley, potatoes, sheep and salt fish. Dr Marshall says that, up to 90 tons of barley was being exported to Scotland annually. This would have been used in whisky distilling. He says that "the land is divided into small farms. Each house has a garden for vegetables, which is well enclosed against sheep or cattle. The remainder is planted in barley, potatoes and oats. There is some flax grown and, on the farms of Mr Gage and Mr McDonnell in Ouig, wheat is grown."

He also mentions potato gardens along the shore, below the white cliffs. " Nearly every family has a small flock they graze in common, with each owner's mark on them."

Dr Marshall arrived in Ballycastle at 7 pm on Friday, 27th June 1834. He found that a boat had just arrived from the island with a load of potatoes. The crew did not intend returning until the following morning. He, however, persuaded them to take him to the island the same evening. They left Ballycastle at 8 o'clock and had to row most of the way. He says it was a fine evening, with the sun setting below the waves. Having arrived on the island, the boatmen took him to the public house, where he found accommodation. It had only been opened within the previous few years. He was highly pleased with his first night on Rathlin, having joined the locals in the bar for a drink and listened to some traditional

Rathlin songs in Irish. One was sung by two men as a duet, and lasted fifteen minutes, everyone joining in the chorus. Rathlin has an ancient tradition of music and singing, which still exists today, though unfortunately the Gaelic has been lost.

The boatmen who brought him over were from Kenramer. He visited them the following week. When he was at Cleggan Lough, they were working at peat in the moss in Bealach an Sluaigh (the road or way of the fairies). He noted their flock of sheep and herd of cattle, grazing in the valley to the south of the houses. The animals grazed together and although belonging to eight or ten families, each one had their owner's mark. He notes that "the tradesmen on the island are two or three tailors and shoemakers and a few boat builders, the people use their own wool and flax for woolen and linen clothing. They plait straw hats. There is a shop for groceries and some medicines".

In an account of fishing, he says that the glashan or Coal fish was formerly caught in large numbers, salted and exported but, in the 1830's, had become scarce. "They had once been so numerous that a boat could be filled with them in Church Bay, using only a boat hook. Cod are also scarcer, the only cod bank being Skirnaw, between Rathlin and Islay. Lythe are plentiful and often weigh up to seven pounds. Herring are also scarce, but others such as skate, ling, gurnard and murron or wrasse, plaice and turbot are plentiful. Lobster are very plentiful, although it seems to be boats from Dublin or Liverpool that are catching them." He says that, using twenty or thirty baskets or creels, they frequently took two or three lobsters from each one in a morning. "The boats stay two or three days and, having a good catch, head off to the markets with them."

It is curious that the fishing industry has never developed on Rathlin as it has in Donegal and the west of Scotland. Campbeltown, on the Mull of Kintyre, which is twelve miles distant from Rathlin, had a substantial fishing industry in the second half of the 19th century. Perhaps the lack of a safe harbour, which could hold bigger boats, was the main problem for the island.

Rathlin did not suffer from the clearances, as the Scottish islands did during this period when people were forcibly removed from their land holdings and replaced with sheep. There were three townlands where the people were removed to other holdings and replaced with sheep. They were Kebble, Kilpatrick and Ballynagard. The people were moved out of Kebble in the 1850s to other holdings on the island. Amongst those removed were my great grandparents, Augustine and Elizabeth McCurdy. They were given land in Ballygill South, known as Garvagh (the rough field) about 1850.

Apart from these events, the 40 or so years from 1800 were the most stable for several centuries, but it was not to last. During the previous 100 years the population of Ireland and the Highlands of Scotland, as well as the northern part of England, had become almost totally dependent on the potato as a staple food. In Ireland there were several reasons for this. The potato would grow on land where grain would not. The policy of the plantation of Ireland had driven the native population into the worst land, leaving the planters on the best land. The potato was the only crop which would grow successfully on this hill land. There were many uprisings against this policy, and the Crown forces frequently employed a scorched earth policy against the people. It was not quite so easy to burn a potato crop. All these factors, plus an increasing population, left the people very dependent on one crop, the potato.

The potato blight first appeared in the summer of 1845 in Germany, France, the Netherlands, Belgium and the south of England. The first reports of its arrival in Ireland was contained in Irish newspapers on 6th September, 1845. It was reported in the Lisburn, Antrim, Ballymoney and Ballycastle areas. However, as it was late in the year, many areas escaped it. The following year, 1846, saw the blight take hold. By the month of July, most of the potato crop was already destroyed. This marked the beginning of the famine years.

There were other economic factors which contributed to the disaster. One of these was the collapse of the rural weaving industry, caused by mechanisation which concentrated weaving in large towns, such as Belfast. In previous decades weaving in the cottages had provided a small regular income which carried people over hard times. On Rathlin nearly every house had a weaving loom. When this source of income disappeared there was no alternative income, but the rents still had to be paid. The only resource left was the grain crops - oats and barley, and some wheat. Due to the collapse of the potato crop in western Europe, grain was fetching high prices in England. The tenants paid their rent in grain. The Landlords (many of whom were absent) exported this grain to England for the high prices. This enabled them to continue to lead the 'Life of Reilly', regardless of the needs of their tenants.

It is worth noting here that potato blight is endemic in western Europe, Britain and Ireland to the present day. It is kept under control by regular spraying with chemicals from early June each year. It does not appear possible at present to develop strains of seed which are blight resistant. Perhaps this may come in the future with genetic engineering, although this process is highly controversial at present.

The export of grain left very little for the people to survive on. Famine was the inevitable result. Rathlin's Landlord at the time, Rev. Robert Gage, applied to the Government for assistance under the Poor Employment Act. Under this Act, public works were undertaken, e.g. drainage. Those employed were paid a subsistence wage. There is no record of it being extended to Rathlin. Mr Gage was appointed a member of the Finance Committee for Ballycastle District. From this, a Rathlin Island Relief Committee was set up. However, this committee soon resigned, owing to the Government's refusal to alter the rules to suit the peculiar circumstances of Rathlin as an island.

Mr Gage wrote to Mr Bernard McManus, the Government Relief Inspector for Ballycastle, stating that he would be willing to subscribe the equivalent of a shilling rate, about £40, saying that he had already allowed the people to use for food what would normally have paid the rent. This, of course, was the grain grown on the island. Mr McManus replied to this letter, saying that the Commissioners had ordered the Commissary General to give £40 worth of provisions out of the funds placed in his hands by the British Association. Secondly, an amount equivalent to Mr Gage's subscription and thirdly, there was £10 or £15 more subscribed by other parties. Totalling this up, he said there would be about £63 coming from the Government in addition to Mr Gage's subscription.

On 25th May, 1847, Thomas G Folingsby wrote to Robert Gage, stating that he had received Mr Gage's cheque for £50 from the Master of the sloop "Annie", with which he purchased 32 barrels of Indian corn meal, American ground, at 31 shillings per barrel. This totalled £49/12 shillings. In addition he purchased 3 tons of Carolina rice at £28/10 shillings per ton and 2 tons of broken Patna rice at £25 per ton. The bill for the rice to be sent to Mr Bernard McManus at Ballycastle. Altogether it appears that grain and rice, to the value of £103/12 shillings was purchased for Rathlin and shipped on the sloop "Annie".

There is a story that I recall hearing my father and Mickey Joe Anderson talking about, concerning another ship called "Erin's Hope" coming to the island with American Indian corn meal. This meal was sent to Rathlin by the emigrants from the island who had left in the early years, before the famine. Several other donations were given to the Landlord, particularly for the purchase of new seed for the following year.

There was a ship came ashore on July 24th, 1847, at the Bull Point. This was the "Saracen" and she is supposed to have had a cargo of flour on board. According to the stories of the time, most of this cargo was saved by the islanders and every home got a share of it. This period was a watershed in Rathlin's history. Emigration started in earnest. In the decade from 1841 to 1851 the population dropped from 1010 to 753, a decrease of 257 and in the next decade, to 1861, there was a further drop of 300 to 453. This was a dramatic loss of people over 20 years.

Some went to Belfast for work, some to Greenock and Glasgow on Clydeside in Scotland and obtained work in the shipyards. There was at the time, and for many years afterwards, a shipyard on the Clyde under the name of McCurdy. This yard was supposed to have been founded by former emigrants from Rathlin.

Three of my grandfather's brothers, Alec, Augustine and John McCurdy, went to work on the Clyde as ships' carpenters in the 1860s. Many other islanders went to America on the emigration ships. There is a record of negotiations between Robert Gage and the J & J Cooke Shipping Line of Derry in 1847, for the transport of eighty or more people from Rathlin to America. In the spring of 1847 there were 107 people who left the island. There is no mention in the shipping lists of J & J Cooke of taking these people, so they must have sailed on another Line.

The 'Charles Napier' sailed from Derry in 1847 for St. John in New Brunswick, Canada. Listed as passengers are Donal, James and Mary Black, Mary McFaul and John McCurdy all from Rathlin and James, Nelly, Kitty and Mary McCurdy of Ballycastle, also Archibald McCurdy of Ballycastle and James and Nancy Black of Rathlin.

In 1848 the 'Lord Maidstone' sailed for St. John and lists Betty and Mary McFaul of Rathlin as passengers. I have not been able to discover any other passenger lists with Rathlin names. What we do know from American records is that almost all Rathlin emigrants settled in northern Maine, around Lubec, Eastport, Pembroke and Perry. This is the most easterly part of the United States and is sixty miles or so across the border from St. John in New Brunswick. It is likely that the emigrants preferred to be under the government of the United States rather than the colonial government of Canada.

I am indebted to Patricia Townsend (nee McCurdy), formerly of Lubec, for a great deal of information and records of Rathlin people and their descendants in the Lubec and Eastport areas. Patricia and her husband visited Rathlin in 1993. More recently I met John B Craig, formerly of Pembroke near Lubec, and his wife Sue. They visited Rathlin in 1996. He has also given me a great deal of information on Rathlin people who settled around Pembroke. John's great grandparents, Neil and Catherine Craig were from Ballygill North, Rathlin and went to Pembroke in 1853.

Many of the emigrants found employment in the Pembroke ironworks, which was established in 1832. They worked twelve hour shifts. The day men started at six o'clock in the morning, with the night men starting at six in the evening. John Craig has supplied me with lists of Rathlin natives in the Pembroke area from Census data for the years 1850, 1860, 1870, 1880, 1900 and 1920. These lists I am including for the historical interest. It will be noticed that by 1920 almost all of the Rathlin natives have died out. Their descendants would, of course, be classified as born in the United States.

By the year 1861, emigration from Rathlin had slowed down considerably. The Landlord re-distributed the land amongst the remaining tenants. The General Valuation of Rateable Property in Ireland of 1861 lists the following information:

Alexander McDonnell is listed as owning 47 acres in Demesne, 45 acres in Ballynoe and 9 acres in Church Quarter, plus the store in Ushet port and the corn mill in Kinkeel. The Ballast Board i.e. the forerunners of The Commissioners of Irish Lights owns the land where the East Lighthouse and keepers' houses stand in Ballycarry. James McFaul owns a house in Mullindress, which is let to

Rev. Michael McCartney, the Priest on the island. The remainder of the island is held by the Gage family on long lease from the McDonnells of Antrim. There are 75 tenants renting land from Robert Gage. There are no tenants in Cabbal, Kilpatrick and Ballynagard.

### Tenancies

Kinramer North had four tenants; Kinramer South, 2 tenants; Cleggan, 4 tenants; Ballygill North, 3 tenants; Ballygill Middle, 5 tenants; Ballygill South 3 tenants; Knockans, 4 tenants. These 25 tenants were renting 1319 acres, i.e. an average holding of 53 acres each.

Ballyconagan had 6 tenants; Ballycarry, 9 tenants; Criagmacagan, 7 tenants; Demesne, 5 tenants; Mullindress, 1 tenant; Roonivoolin, 4 tenants; Kinkeel, 5 tenants; Ballynoe 2 tenants; Carrivindoon, 7 tenants and Carrivinally, 4 tenants. These 50 tenants were renting 1357 acres, giving an average holding of 27 acres.

### Ploughing with Horses

These 75 tenancies represented approximately 450 people. This much reduced population, having more land per tenant, were able to have an improved standard of living. Although much of the available land was rough grazing, each tenant had between five and ten acres of arable ground, for crops of corn, barley, potatoes and beans. From this time onwards, ploughing the land with horses became the general method of cultivation, right up until the 1950s, when the Ferguson tractor took over. The disadvantage with using horses for farm work was that the horses ate most of the crops produced, the rest going to feed the cattle. And so the number of cattle kept was governed by the necessity to keep the horses well fed, and so much of the years' work went into growing enough to feed the horses which did the ploughing and carting. This cycle was eventually broken by the invention of the tractor.

### Land Reform

In the decades following the famine, there developed considerable tenant agitation for land reform, as the existing system in Ireland of land tenure and absent landlords, was seen as an evil which contributed in great measure to the cause of the famine.

This movement was started in 1847 by John Mitchel, an Ulster Presbyterian who was involved with the Young Irelanders, a movement associated with Daniel O'Connell, 'The Liberator', who died in Genoa, Italy on 15th May 1847.

John Mitchel was arrested in May, 1848, on a charge of sedition and was sentenced to transportation to Australia. Despite these setbacks, the agitation for reform continued until 1879, when the cause was taken up by Michael Davitt, whose family had been evicted from their land holding in Co. Mayo and finished up in Lancashire. He formed the Land League and Charles Stewart Parnell was its first President.

## Michael Davitt

This movement gathered momentum and within a year was holding meetings throughout Ireland. In November, 1880, a meeting was held in Ballycastle. As the day was stormy, islanders were not able to get to Ballycastle, however, there were a few islanders at the meeting. This pressure from the Land League led to a succession of land purchase Acts by the Government in 1881, 1885, 1891 and 1903. These various Acts made it progressively easier for tenants to buy their freehold, with the Government advancing the purchase price, which was repayable over a number of years. By the year 1910, 300,000 tenants had purchased their freehold. The rent for Rathlin before the Land Act of 1881 was £800. Shortly afterwards the rent was reduced to £519/7s.

## Land Court

In April 1907, 54 tenants from Rathlin entered the Land Court to have their rents fixed at a fair level. They were assisted in this by the island Priest, Fr. E McGowan and a Belfast solicitor, Francis Joseph Bigger. The Land Court reduced the rent to £334/3s., fixed for fifteen years. This decision was appealed by the Landlord and in October, 1908 the Chief Land Commission fixed the rents at £340/2s/6d, an increase of £5/19s/6d. Following the Partition of Ireland in 1922, the two separate administrations introduced legislation making the sale of estates compulsory.

## Land Purchase Commission

In Northern Ireland this was known as the Northern Ireland Land Act 1925 and the provisions of the Act were carried out by the Land Purchase Commission. Under this legislation the land of Rathlin was vested in the Land Commission. The Landlord was paid a fair valuation and the existing tenants commenced to purchase the freehold from the Land Commission in 1931. Repayments were spread over a number of years, usually 30 or 35. During this period and the decade following, prices for cattle, sheep and cereal crops reached their lowest ebb of this century and, although the purchase price of the land was set at a very reasonable level, many of the former tenants did not find it easy to meet their annual payments.

In the centuries before the 1850s, cultivation was mainly carried out with the spade. On Rathlin much of the land in use was not accessible to a plough or horse, in any case, most tenants could not afford to keep a horse. The landlord kept horses for his own use and there were always a few ponies. Evidence of this spade cultivation can still be seen in many places on the island, in the form of 'rigs'. This is a word which may be Scots Gaelic in origin, I have seen it in writings from the 16th and 17th Centuries. It is a system which is very old and was, in early times, used throughout western Europe for planting crops. It was ideally suited to the potato. Another term which has been used to describe this method of cultivation is 'Lazy-bed', this term was coined by travellers/writers who had no comprehension of the principles underlying this system and who, generally speaking, knew the price of everything and the value of nothing.

Rigs always followed the 'lie' or slope of the land. They ranged in width from four to seven feet. The spade length was used as a measure. Generally the wide rigs were on drier ground. The method of making rigs was firstly to divide the plot into the widths preferred. Farmyard manure or seaweed was then spread and lastly soil was dug from trenches each side and thrown on top of the manure. The rig was then left until it was time to plant the potatoes. Early crops were planted around 17th March, St. Patrick's Day. This is within a few days of the vernal Equinox, when the temperature starts to rise. The main crop was planted in early May. The method of planting was to make a hole with a stick and drop the seed in. There were a couple of advantages to this system. Firstly, they could be prepared during any dry spell of weather in the early Spring. Secondly, the trenches served for drainage, allowing the rig to warm up more quickly in the early Spring sunshine.

## Common Grazing

There was no security of tenure. The Ordnance Survey of 1830 states that each year, lots were drawn to decide who would occupy land the next year. Many of the strips so allocated were no more than an eighth of an acre and were held alternately by each tenant in a townland. Another system which prevailed was common grazing throughout the island between Michaelmas or Hallowe'en and St. Patrick's Day (31st October until 17th March).

## Walls and Road Building

Townland dividing walls were built from 1780 onwards but it was not until the 1860s onwards that walls were built to divide farms and fields. Stones were obtained from dwellings that were abandoned when their owners emigrated. Much stone was also quarried. Field dividing walls of basalt were built as a single course wall, ranging from three feet up to five feet high. The stones were not dressed or faced, but built as found. There was a considerable degree of skill in this work and each winter the farmer would go around the walls, replacing any stones that had been knocked off by cattle. When moving animals from one field to another a small section of wall was taken down and then rebuilt. This gap was known as a 'slap', a word with origins in the Irish language. Gates were not in

Townlands of Glebe and Demense. Note fields cultivated and carrying a range of crops. In the foreground is the Church of Ireland Glebe Hall. Beyond it the large house with two chimneys is Ballynoe House, the McDonnell House.
Photograph by Alex Hogg, about 1915

This is an excellent photograph by Alex Hogg, about 1915, showing the station pier, the former coastguard station houses, the coastguard boathouse and further along the beach, the kelp store, still with roof on and in use at the time as a coal store by Neil McCuaig. Note the cultivated fields and the tidy limestone walls and round gate pillars. The white roads are of limestone gravel from the beach.

use, except by the Landlord and his own farmland. Many of the well-built circular gate pillars can still be seen in the fields adjacent to the harbour. They are built mainly of limestone quarried in the area. These pillars were built by the stone masons brought in by the Landlord. Most of the walls in this area were built by masons, assisted by island men. Many of the walls and pillars can be seen in photographs included at the back of this book.

The use of stone on Rathlin for building dates back to the Neolithic period. Foundations from that time can still be seen. The Neolithic people were able to use very large rocks. In the foundations still existing there are stones which would be a ton and more in weight. In more modern times, very large stones were used in the construction of buildings, particularly the corner stones. It is my belief that these same stones have been re-used many times over thousands of years.

Division of the island by stone walls was started by the Landlord about 1780. The first walls were the townland boundaries and these can still be seen today. The individual fields were the next to be walled in, although a good deal of arable land was in the rundale system and was never walled.

The roads on the island were no more than tracks over the hills up until 1780. In the 1770s Robert Gage was Chairman of the Grand Jury of Co. Antrim. The Grand Jury consisted of the principal landlords of the County and was the forerunner of County Councils. They were empowered to require the personal labour of tenants in the construction of roads. This power led to widespread unrest, as some landlords abused the system and had roads built in their own lands.

Road building on Rathlin commenced in 1783, when a main road from Cabbal to the Rue was started. This was a very considerable task, particularly from Church Quarter to Cabbal. There is no record of how many men worked on the road building but a vast amount of quarrying and carting stone was required to complete the task.

**Rathlin in the Charts**

Rathlin's situation, in a busy seaway between Ireland and Scotland, has meant that it has presented a hazard to seafarers throughout recorded history and no doubt before records were kept. Rathlin is shown on marine charts of the 14th and 15th Centuries which were drawn by Venetian map makers. There must have been considerable trading between the Mediterranean ports and the Irish sea ports to have warranted the inclusion of Rathlin on the charts. No doubt many ships were wrecked in those far off days. We know of many shipwrecks in more modern times. Through the 19th and early 20th Centuries sailing ships were much more difficult to control than modern ships.

## East Lighthouse

All trans-Atlantic shipping from Glasgow, Liverpool and Belfast passed by Rathlin. However, it was not until the 1850s that the island got its first Lighthouse. The first recorded application for a light on Rathlin was in 1827, but due to a difference of opinion between the Ballast Board in Dublin and the Commissioners of Northern Lights in Edinburgh, it was not until 1847 that final approval was given by Trinity House for Rathlin East Lighthouse.

Construction started in May 1849, to a design by Inspector George Halpin and carried out by the Ballast Board's own workmen. Incidentally, the Ballast Board was the forerunner of today's Commissioners of Irish Lights. The tower and other buildings, including the former keepers' houses, are all built from stone quarried on the island, although the window sills etc. are of granite, which was likely cut and dressed in Dublin and shipped to Rathlin. The Lighthouse finally came to life on the 1st November, 1856, with an upper flashing and lower fixed light. This lower fixed light was discontinued on 1st July, 1894. The flashing light showed a red sector on the line of Carrick-a-Vann reef off Kenbane Head on the Antrim coast. This was finally discontinued in 1938. On 18th January 1866, a fog signal was established, which consisted of an 18 pounder gun fired every 20 minutes during foggy weather. Over the years the frequency was reduced to 15 minutes, then 8 minutes and, in 1918, to a double explosion every 5 minutes. The fog signal was finally discontinued in 1972.

Originally the light was an acetylene generator. This was changed in 1912 to a vaporised paraffin burner and finally, in 1981, to electric power. The tower exterior was originally natural stone with a broad red band painted under the balcony. Then the stone was painted white, still with the red band. Finally, the red band was painted black in 1933 and so it remains today. The explosive fog signal gave rise to at least one accident, as recorded by Jim Dillon in Beam magazine 1997-98, published by the Marine Department on behalf of the Commissioners of Irish Lights, Dublin.

Jim relates how a friend of his family, Denny Duff, was stationed at Rathlin East when the steamer 'Princess Maud' was passing Rathlin on an excursion from Belfast. The keepers thought it would be a nice gesture to fire a salute. The charge misfired and as Denny Duff was reloading there was still some smoldering remains of the first charge in the gun. The second charge exploded prematurely and shattered Denny's arm. The keepers signalled a White Star Liner, Liverpool bound. They sent a boat ashore and picked up Denny. He was taken to hospital in Liverpool, where part of his arm was amputated. This, of course, ended his days in the Lighthouse service.

Rathlin East was a lively place. There were six keepers' houses and the married keepers had their families with them. The children attended the Rathlin school and, of course, there was the occasional party. I can recall attending parties at the East. Those days have gone now, all Lighthouses in Ireland are automatic, controlled by computer, no parties with computers!

### Rathlin West Lighthouse

Although Rathlin East Lighthouse made a vast contribution to safety at sea, it could not be seen by ships approaching from a westerly direction, so requests were again made for a Lighthouse at the west end of Rathlin. An inspecting committee visited the island. Differences of opinion were expressed between Trinity House and Irish Lights over which point was most suitable, whether Bull Point or Crockantirrive. It was suggested that the light could be on one and the fog signal on the other. Eventually Crockantirrive was chosen and the Board of Trade sanctioned it in 1904. Five years elapsed before the subject was brought up again and the Board agreed to include the whole project in its estimates for 1910-11. Work first got under way in 1912, under the supervision of designer, Mr Scott.

The first major task was to build an inclined railway, and small pier with derrick at Cooraghy. When the wagons were loaded off the supply ship they were hauled, via the inclined railway to the top of a 200 foot cliff by means of a large underground winch, which was wound up by four horses walking a circle pulling a shaft. A road had also to be quarried and built across Cabbal to bring the building material by horse and cart to the top of Crockantirrive. Another vast undertaking was to quarry out the platform, where the lighthouse stands. I heard my grandfather say that this was all done by hand, as Mr Scott was against doing any blasting, in case it shook up the whole cliff face.

Progress was slow, but by the end of 1916, the light and accommodation for keepers was completed. However, because the First World War was in progress, it was not until 10th March, 1919, that the light was brought into operation. This is a red flash every five seconds, the only red light on the Irish coast. The reason was to distinguish it from all other lights which can be seen from a ship coming in from the Atlantic. My grandfather, Sean McNearney, was general foreman on the construction. He brought his family from Belfast and they lived in a wooden house at the top of Cooraghy for six years. The foundations are still there. The cost of building the lighthouse was an unbelievable amount of over £400,000. However, it no doubt prevented many shipwrecks. A fog signal was not brought into operation until 15th July, 1925. It was operated on compressed air. The Lighthouse went automatic on 30th November, 1983, and so the keepers were no longer stationed there.

### The Rue Lighthouse

In July, 1914 an unmanned light was recommended by the Inspecting Committee of Irish Lights and by 19th November, 1915 a temporary light was brought into service without the customary Notice to Mariners being issued. This was to prevent German submariners making use of the information. However, the temporary light only survived two years, being wrecked in a storm in November, 1917 and so the light was transferred to the undamaged fog gun trestle, which had come into operation on 12th April, 1917.

When weather conditions required the use of the fog gun, two keepers were on duty, living in a wooden hut which was finally dismantled a few years ago. The fog gun was acetylene operated, but was not entirely reliable and after a few breakdowns it was finally withdrawn in January, 1931.

The light continued to be operated by a water to carbide acetylene generator until 9th October, 1965, when it was replaced by electric power from a diesel generator. Today it is powered by a wind turbine. Incidentally, Mrs. Letitia Stevenson, wife of the Curate, Leslie Stevenson, gives a graphic account of visiting the Rue in 1921 and seeing work starting on the new, permanent lighthouse and the men breaking stones to build it. There was a fierce storm in November, 1921; mountainous seas washed away all their building materials and the generator house. The hut which the men lived in was under water and the foreman, E J Smith, had a narrow escape as he had been in the generator house minutes before it was washed away. The new stone tower withstood the onslaught and is still there today. In a north west gale it is a spectacular sight to see the seas breaking over it.

### Rathlin Coastguard

The first mention of Coastguards on Rathlin is in 1823, when the houses which comprise the 'Station' were built to house what were then known as Waterguards. The role of these people had little to do with lifesaving, but had a great deal to do with catching smugglers. At this time smuggling was rife all around the coasts of Britain and Ireland. The Waterguards remained on Rathlin for a good many years. By 1856 smuggling had declined considerably and responsibility for the service passed from the Board of Customs to the Admiralty. The Coastguard Service Act came into force that year and remained under their control until after the First World War.

The first modern account of a Coastguard Service on Rathlin dates from 1914. The members of this, about 20, were all volunteers, ready to go out at any time of day or night. They were summoned by the firing of a maroon at what was, and still is, known at the Rocket House. This is where the lifesaving equipment and cart were kept. The cart was large and heavy and was pulled by three horses. As shipwrecks usually happen in remote places where the cart was not able to go, a great deal of carrying of equipment was necessary. When a ship was ashore the first requirement was to get a line across it. This was a light rope. Before 1930 the method of doing this was by a 'heaving cane'. This was a bamboo pole attached to the rope. At the end of the rope was a lead ball which, when thrown out, would hopefully reach the stricken ship. If it did, it would be made fast by the ship's crew and then the breeches buoy was sent out and a crew member would climb into this and be hauled back to the land, mostly through the water. This was repeated until all the crew were safely ashore. An operation like this could be difficult enough in daylight but, at night time on a cliff, it was extremely hazardous. Rathlin Coastguards have a record second to none and have twice been awarded the Board of Trade Wreck Service Shield, in 1930 and 1948.

Perhaps the 'Shackleton' rescue, on the night of 1st March, 1930, was the most outstanding of all the rescues by the Rathlin Life Saving Company. It was nearly 5 p.m. when the Rathlin Life Saving Company set out to Greenan Point, a 200 ft cliff on the north side of the island. The 'Shackleton' was aground in thick fog. The life saving apparatus had to be manhandled across nearly two miles of boggy ground. By this time it was dark and visibility was down to a few yards because of the fog. Assisted by the shouts of the trawler crew, the rescue company

The Fleetwood Trawler, Shackleton, ashore at Greenan Point, Rathlin. It was up the cliff face that the crew were hauled the safety, in darkness and thick fog, by the Rathlin Life Saving Volunteers in 1930. Photograph Northern Whig.

**The Volunteers who rescued the crew of the trawler, Shackleton**

Back row (l to r): Brendan Kelly, Augustine McCurdy (Sen)

Middle row (l to r): Daniel McQuilken, John Curry, Jack McCurdy, Mickey Joe Anderson, Paddy Anderson, Albert Glass, Danny McCuaig, Alex Anderson, John Joe McCurdy, Patrick Black, Paddy Black, Jimmy McCurdy, James McCurdy, John Heggarty, Douglas Cecil, Kevin Black, Robert McCormick, Rev. C.H. O'Hare, Frank McCurdy, Con Maguire, Bob Cecil, Dan Smyth, Robert Black, John McCurdy

Front row (l to r): Joseph Anderson, John McQuilken, Mickey McCuaig, Daniel McKinley, Archie Darragh, John Black, Loughie Black, Owen Murphy, Niel McCuaig, Sandy Maguire, Donal McCurdy began to fire rockets with lines attached. This was the first use of the new rocket lines, but it was not until the sixth rocket that a line was secured to the ship. Then began the business of getting the men to the top of the cliff. There is no beach here, so some of the island men had to climb half way down the cliff to release the crewmen from the breeches buoy. Once on a rocky ledge they were taken up a rope ladder to the cliff top, where they were met by the island Priest, Fr. O'Hare. It was 6 o'clock in the morning when the last of the 14 man crew was at the top of the cliff. After being provided with food and warm clothing, they were picked up by another trawler the following day.

Apart from receiving the National Life Saving Shield, the trawler owners had a marble tablet erected in the Parish Hall. This lists the names of all those involved in the rescue and each man received a scroll, listing the names and a photo of the Shackleton aground.

During the First World War a Coast Watch was set up. There were two teams of four men each. The Upper End team covered the cliffs, north and south, as far as the East Lighthouse. Their names were: James Black of Glacklugh, John Black of Kinraver, Patrick McCurdy of Cleggan and Donal McCurdy of Ballinagard. The Lower End team covered the cliffs from the East Lighthouse to the Rue, both sides of the island. Their names were: Mr Parkist, Head officer from the mainland, Daniel McQuilkin, Ouig; James Glass, Ouig; James Heggarty of the 'Station'. For this service the pay was 14/- (70p) per week. This duty was discontinued in 1918.

In July 1935 another service was set up. This was known as Bad Weather Watch. M J Anderson of Glackanacre was in charge and it was at his discretion that the Watch was called out. This continued until 1940. The names of the men were: M J Anderson, John Joe McCurdy, Daniel McKinley and Daniel McQuilkin.

## Coastguard Lookout

With the outbreak of the Second World War there were further changes. In 1940 the Auxiliary Coastguard was set up, and in 1941-42, a Coastguard lookout hut was built at Cantruan. This gave a good view of the north channel, from the Mull of Kintyre to Malin head. The contractor who built this hut was Arthur McElnay of Dunluce. Islanders who worked at it were John Black of Glacklugh, carpenter; John McQuilkin of Ouig and Bob McKay of Crocknanagh.

The first auxiliary Coastguards were: Duncan Smyth Sen., William McKay, John McQuilkin Sen., Frank McCurdy, Ballinagard. After the 'Loughgarry' sank off the east side with the loss of 29 lives, the number of auxiliaries was increased. These were Daniel McQuilkin, Donal McCurdy, John Joe McCurdy, Ambrose Armstrong (retired Lighthouse keeper), John Cecil Jnr., Albert Glass and John Curry Sen. This service ended at the end of the War in 1945. However, the Coastguard service continues until the present day.

## Marconi

Another facet of safety at sea involved Guglielmo Marconi, who was experimenting with radio signals in the 1890s. In February, 1896, he came to London at the age of 22. In July of that year he was introduced to the Chief Engineer of the Post Office, W H Preece, who had also been experimenting with radio. Marconi continued to carry out experiments in various places, mostly successful.

In May, 1898, Marconi was asked by Lloyds Insurers of London if he could set up a wireless or radio link at Rathlin Island. The reason for this was that Lloyds wished to know, as quickly as possible, that ships insured by them had crossed the Atlantic safely. If they were in view of Rathlin East Lighthouse, then they were in reasonably safe waters. Lloyds had an observation point at Torr Head on the mainland, however, there was great difficulty in getting messages about shipping from Rathlin. They had tried carrier pigeons, but they were frequently taken by the peregrine falcons. Another method in general use at Lighthouses was semaphore, using two white bats. This, of course, was not much use in fog or mist or in the dark.

Marconi sent his assistant, George Kemp, to Rathlin. He engaged the services of a young graduate from Trinity College, Edward Glanville. They set up a transmitter and aerials at the East Lighthouse and a transmitter and receiver at Ballycastle, and, on 6th July, 1898, successfully transmitted the first signals from Rathlin. This was the beginning of regular radio transmissions for commercial purposes anywhere on the Earth.

Young Edward Glanville met with his death on Rathlin, when, on Sunday, 21st August, 1898, he fell from a cliff near the Lighthouse. His body was discovered by John Sullivan, a Lighthouse keeper at the Lighthouse. The only islander employed on this project was Mr John Cecil, of Castle Quarter.

On 25th July, 1998, Marconi's daughter, Princessa Elettra Marconi Giovanelli, visited Rathlin as part of a centenary commemoration.

## Employment on Rathlin

The first two decades of the 20th century saw quite a lot of construction work on Rathlin. There was the West Lighthouse, the 'North' or 'Manor House' pier, Killeaney limestone quarry and the Rue Lighthouse. All of this construction brought a good deal of money into the island. Many islanders were employed on the contracts, houses were improved, some had roofs slated for the first time. By the early 1920s these contracts were finished, only Killeaney limestone quarry was still going.

I include a pay sheet from 20th September, 1924, the name is Black. I am not sure if the initial is G or P. It can be seen that the rate of pay was £1/7/6d for 44 hours work - 7.5 pence per hour in today's money - £1 37.5p per week, or about 4p per hour. Not a fortune but, of course, there was no unemployment benefit in those days. Incidentally, this old money system was discontinued on 14th February, 1971.

| RATHLIN LIMESTONE CO. | | | | |
|---|---|---|---|---|
| WEEK SHEET. | | | | |
| Name G Black | Week ending Sept 20 192 4 | | | |
| | Overburden | Quarrying | Loading | Drilling |
| MONDAY | 8 6 | – | — | — |
| TUESDAY | 8 6 | – | — | — |
| WEDNESDAY | — | — | 4, 6 | — |
| THURSDAY | 8 6 | – | — | — |
| FRIDAY | 8 6 | – | — | |
| SATURDAY | 4 6 | – | — | — |

44 Hours per Week
Rate of Pay 7½ d

Remarks:— Wheeling out

Overburden 3 6 6        1  2  6
Quarrying
Loading 4 6            —  2  6
Drilling
        4, 6        —  2  6
                £ 1 · 7 · 6

In 1924 a Coleraine company, Gaston & Son, purchased the wreck 'Drake' from the Admiralty and started salvage operations in the month of June, 1924. The 'Drake' was a 14,000-ton heavy cruiser which had been torpedoed off Rathlin on 2nd October, 1916, and sank in Church Bay, Rathlin. Some islanders were employed on this work. However, problems arose over the rates of pay. On 24th July, 1924, Gaston & Son wrote to Mr W S Johnston in Northumberland, who owned the Killeaney quarry and quite a bit of land on the island. Gaston's problem was that his employees were asking for a pay rise to 1/- per hour (5p). Gaston laid the blame for this on one employee, John McFee Jnr. Now this young McFee was the son of John McFee Snr., who managed the limestone quarry. Gastons labelled him as the ringleader and moreover, that he was living in a house belonging to Mr Johnston. Clearly, Gastons were trying to draw Johnston into the dispute. All of the men, both salvage and quarry men, were members of the Amalgamated Transport and General Workers' Union, with offices at 9, Queens Square, Belfast.

A letter from the Union, dated 23rd July, 1924, to Mr Gaston at Rathlin, informed him that, owing to the attitude taken by him regarding the salvage workers, the Union will have no alternative but to refuse to handle any materials belonging to Gaston at any port in the UK. He asks Gaston to pay the men time and a half for all overtime. This letter from the Union was signed by Laughlin McCurdy, who was the National organiser, and who had, and still has, relatives on Rathlin. This Laughlin McCurdy later was an Alderman of Belfast City Council.

On 31st July, 1924, a further letter from Gaston to Johnston thanks him for his letter dated the 28th. Seemingly, Johnston has misunderstood Gaston's remarks regarding McFee. Possibly Johnston did not want to get involved with the Gaston's problems over pay rates. However, Gaston says that the men have just informed him that their Union Secretary has advised them to return to work until he arrives on Rathlin. Gaston says that this means he will have to give an advance, presumably at the increased rate. He asks Johnston to take no further action until after the arrival of the Union Secretary.

The letters do not state the final outcome, however, as with all such pay disputes, no one gets all they want, so presumably there was a satisfactory settlement. I am grateful to Ian McClean for this information. Of course, the John McFee Sen. referred to as quarry manager was Ian's grandfather and the house was Bridge House, which still belongs to Ian's family. Killeaney Quarry finally closed down in 1927.

Another source of income had been the kelp burning. Good prices had prevailed during the 1914-18 war - £20 to £24 per ton. In 1920 the price was £16 per ton and continued to fall to the point when no one gathered it. The last was gathered around 1930. Dulse (dilisk) continued to be gathered in small amounts and still is today. There is always a small market for it at the Lammas Fair every August in Ballycastle, although I have recently been told by a food processing company in Belfast that there is now an increasing demand by restaurants and even as far away as Japan. Who knows, there may yet be a great future for Rathlin dulse!

## Boats and Tides

Boats and tides have always been a prominent feature of living on Rathlin. From the earliest times livestock and grain were taken out by boat and all supplies including horses and cows brought in by the same method. The earliest known

This photograph of Joe Brown of Tonduff is by Robert Welch, date uncertain. Joe and his brother, John, fished around Rathlin in the springtime and slept in the caves at Oweyberne. Information supplied by Danny Morgan, Ballycastle. Fisherman identified by Sammy Gault, Dunseverick.

This photograph taken at Cooraghy by Robert Welch 1890. The boat is a clinker built twenty foot. Note the large mainsail and jib. This was a rig used in regattas for racing. As with all Welch's photographs, they are of excellent quality, but are notably composed as if in a studio. The bow anchor rope can be seen and a boat would not have sat at anchor on a lee shore with sails set. Everyone is remarkably well dressed. This is close to the jetty built in 1912 by Irish Lights to unload building materials.

boats were those in use at the time of Columcille. They were made of either horse or cow hides sewn together and stretched over a light wooden framework. Then, in the Ninth and Tenth Centuries, a new type of boat appeared in these waters. This was the Viking longship. They were built with overlapping boards, with a very high bow and stern. This method of building is nowadays known as 'clinker built'. This type of ship was adapted in later centuries by the McDonalds of the Isles and in the 14th, 15th and 16th Centuries became the McDonald war galley that was propelled by oar and sail and could carry up to 100 armed men. These boats were lightly built and, with 10 oars per side, could skim very fast over the water. They did not need harbours, they could be run up onto any convenient beach or even a stony shore. Apart from their use as war galleys, they were used to transport livestock and freight between Scotland and Ireland and among the islands, including Rathlin.

The power of the McDonald's declined in the 17th and 18th Centuries and residents of Rathlin had to rely more on their own resources. There were, by this time, no trees on the island and so boat building reverted to a very ancient type - the currach, the boat of Columcille's time, covered in animal hides. This type of boat is still to be found on the west coast of Ireland, although the skin or covering is now of tarred canvas. The building of these boats has been taken to a high degree of perfection on the Dingle peninsula in Co. Kerry. This is the 'naevog' or canoe which is about 26 ft long and 4 ft 6ins wide.

## Boat builders

Around the end of the 18th and early 19th century a different type of boat began to appear along the north coast. This was a wooden clinker built boat which had its origins in Norway. Ships trading from Norway, bringing timber and barrels of tar, started to bring in a few of these boats on deck, for sale to anyone who needed one. This type of boat building was taken up and developed on the north coast. The oldest of these boat builders still in existence is McDonalds of Moville. This firm was founded by James McDonald in 1750 and is still carried on by the same family today. McDonalds started building in Greencastle, but moved to Moville about 1800. Another family who built boats in Moville were the brothers William and Archie Beattie; their last boat was about 1946. In Portrush, James Hopkins built boats in the early years of the 20th Century. James Kelly, who had been an apprentice with Hopkins, also built boats up until the early 1950s. There were a few others who built the odd boat, including on Rathlin. All of these boats were built light and strong. They had to be light to handle as they were nearly always hauled up above high water after every use.

**The Kelly Family of Coolnacrock "Cul na Cnoc"**
**(l to r): Bob Kelly, Ann Jane "Tot" Kelly, Bob Titterton from the salvage ship**
**"Bouncer", Charlie Kelly, Davy Kelly, John Kelly (sen), Brendan Kelly**
**Photograph about 1921, courtesy of Loughie McQuilkin**

**Northern Whig photograph taken in 1938 after an aeroplane had landed supplies**
**when the Island was stormbound. (l to r): Annie Cecil, Castlequarter; Lizzie**
**McMullan, Station Houses; Bella McQuilkin, Station Houses; Mary McCurdy**
**(nee Thompson), Ouig; Rev. Fr. Maloney; Ann Jane Kelly ("Tot", later**
**McQuilkin); Margaret Anderson (over 90), Station Houses; Nurse McMillan (later**
**McQuilkin), District Nurse; Courtesy of Loughie McQuilkin**

## Island Boat Ports

On Rathlin the ports used, particularly in the Upper End, did not have any safe anchorage. A boat could not be left overnight. There were five boat ports in use at the beginning of the 20th century, Cooraghy was the furthest west and was beside the pier built by Irish Lights. A boat could be hauled up into the cove if bad weather was expected. Oweyberne had two ports, the east or main one and the west port. Below Garvagh, beside the waterfall was safe for a boat, and Killeaney was the most easterly. Before the days of motor boats there was an advantage in keeping boats in these ports. They were nearer the fishing grounds off Bull Point and so less rowing or sailing was required.

Indeed I can recall that the present main harbour on Rathlin was not used a great deal by Upper End boats. As a youngster I have gone directly from Oweyberne and Killeaney to Ballycastle and back by the same route on either the Cleggan boat or the Brockley boat. Oweyberne was the most accessible of these ports. A horse and slipe could be taken down almost to the boat, and any heavy merchandise put on the slipe and taken up out of the port to Cleggan, Glacklugh, Garvagh, Glackanacre or Brockley, or indeed any of the Upper End townlands. The old cart or slipe roads can still be seen through the heather. A slipe was like a large sledge, between five and seven feet long and three or five feet wide. The runners were about six or seven inches high and shod with hoop iron. They would slide easily on grass and were used for many jobs on hilly ground where a cart could not be taken.

The most common size of boat was either 20 ft or 22 ft x 6 ft beam. In the 1920s they were built for £1 per foot. In these days it seems a small amount of money, however, usually a loan had to be taken out with the bank to buy them. A boat of this size could be crewed by 2 or 3 men and even hauled up the beach. The places where they were hauled was regularly cleared of stones washed in by the sea. As mentioned earlier, some boats were built on the island. One such boat was built by my grandmother's father, Michael 'Jack' Anderson of Glackanacre. He built it in the field known as Glaic an Toigh Allais "the hollow of the sweat house, just between Garvagh and Glackanacre. When the 24ft boat was finished, he launched it, with the help of the neighbours and all the net hauling ropes that could be found. The cliff here is about 250 feet high. There is a grassy "inean" or way down to the sea, and it was here that the boat was slid down to the water. Michael 'Jack' got the nickname of 'Noah', when he was building the boat, the hammering could be heard all over the island.

To return to the boats in general use in the 1930s and 40s, many families had an interest or share in a boat. There was only one boat sailing on a regular basis from the island. This was known as the Lighthouse boat. They had a contract with Irish Lights to carry Light keepers and supplies to the island. This was a larger boat, about 28 ft and with a good engine. They sailed every other Tuesday

Carrying 24 days mails from Jack Coyles mail boat in February 1938. The Island had been cut off for 24 days due to storms.
(l to r): Alec McCurdy, Crockaharnan; Jack Coyles, Ballycastle; Dougal McMullan, Station Houses; Neil McCuaig, Demense; Albert Glass, Ouig.
Photograph Northern Whig, courtesy of Loughie McQuilkin

Unloading turf at Station Pier, Rathlin about 1900.
(l to r): Joseph McCurdy, my grandfather; John Black (behind mast), grandfather of Mary and Frances Black; Joseph "Michael Jack" Anderson, my grandmother's brother. Note the horse standing quietly in the water. The boat was known as "The Garvagh Boat". It was bought in Campbeltown, Scotland from people called Brodie, formerly Bradley of Rathlin. They left about 1870.
The young boy is unknown.

This photograph by Robert Welch 1890. Note the Station Pier in the foreground is still the original surface. It was concreted and back wall added some 20 years later. In the background, the wall fronting the Manor House is its only protection from the sea. The present concrete road and pier were not built until some 25 years later. There are very few trees on the braes behind the Manor House, and no houses between it and St. Thomas's Church, just out of the picture on the left.

Loading cattle to be transported to the mainland in the 1970s. Each beast had its legs tied and was "slipped" into the open boat. A boat of this type would often accommodate 5 full-grown cattle.
(l to r): Alec McCurdy (back), Johnny Curry, Peter McCurdy, Sylvie McMullan, Peter McMullan, Loughie McQuilkin., Neal McFaul, J.J. McCurdy, Dominic McCurdy, Maurice McCurdy, Paddy McQuilkin, Tony McCuaig

and islanders who had business or needed to get to Ballycastle for shopping, would go on the Lighthouse boat. The crew and owners were James 'John Beag' McCurdy, Cleggan; John Joe McCurdy, the Station and James McCurdy Jnr., Kinkeel. In later years James 'John Beag' and John Joe retired and were replaced by Paddy McQuilkin, Ouig and Sean McCurdy, Cleggan. The post was brought in by Johnny Coyles of Ballycastle. His contract with the Post Office was for 104 journeys per year. In the 1930s his son Jack took over and the Post days were increased to three, i.e. Monday, Wednesday and Friday. Both Jack and his father sailed boats built by Kelly of Portrush. The Coyles also brought in stores for the island's two shops, which at that time were owned by Annie McCuaig, Demesne, and Mary Jane Hunter of the Station. The Post Office was run by Mrs Mary McCurdy (nee Anderson) in the house which is now The Rathlin Guest House. Upon her retirement Mrs McMullan of the Glebe took it on. In the 1970s Mrs Mary McFaul of the Station took on the Post Office and retired from it in 1999. It is now run by Mr Michael Cecil.

By the 1970s there were fewer boats and they were operated from the Station harbour. In 1975 a much larger boat, a 44 ft fully decked trawler, The 'Iona Isle' was bought by two islanders Neil McFaul and Thomas Cecil. This was followed several years later by the first improvements to the harbour. In 1985 the 'Rathlin Venture' arrived at Rathlin. This was a 48-ft fully decked fishing trawler and was owned by Dominic McCurdy, Richard Green, Joseph McQuilkin, Peter McCurdy and Peter McMullan. These two boats provided passenger and freight service for the island until 1996. The 'Iona Isle' also carried the mails, whilst the 'Rathlin Venture' continued to provide the Lighthouse service.

## Ferries and Breakwaters

In 1996 everything changed. A new ferry service was initiated by the Department of Transport. In December ,1996, the new service commenced with a steel hull, car and passenger ferry, operated by Caledonian MacBrayne, the Scottish ferry company. Very considerable improvements were made to the harbour, a new landing slip at the back of the Manor House pier, a large breakwater on top of Lacknakilly reef and a smaller breakwater on Ruenarone reef. At the same time the harbour at Ballycastle was improved with a new large breakwater and landing slip for the Rathlin ferry. Most of the funding for this work came from the European Union in Brussels.

This car ferry has made life a good deal easier. Coal lorries or oil tankers are able to cross to the island and deliver to each house. Previously, heating oil or diesel had to be brought in 45-gallon barrels. These had to be manhandled off the boats and into tractor trailers. The same applied to coal. To load two or three tons of coal into a boat and then to lift it all off again on Rathlin and onto a trailer and then again at home, was a great deal of back breaking work. Livestock are now taken in or out in a cattle or sheep trailer. The roads have been surfaced with bitumen, which is brought in by lorry.

All of these improvements have made life a lot easier, however, parallel with this progress, the population continues to decline. It has now reached its lowest recorded level since 1669. There are just around seventy people resident full time on the island. A few people of vision have talked of a situationwhereby young people could earn a living on the island from Monday to Friday and then, if they wished, go out at weekends to the towns where there is more social activity. This ideal would require the establishment of business activity capable of providing employment throughout the year. Possibly the best prospect is through the medium of information technology. However, this sort of commercial activity is still only at the theory stage.

Another improvement was the construction of six new houses for islanders, by the Northern Ireland Housing Executive. Housing on Rathlin is of a good standard, many of the old houses have been modernised and extended over recent years, and are equivalent to mainland standards. There is however, no surplus housing which could be leased to anyone coming to live on the island.

A further addition was the establishment of a Fire Service in 1989. This is run on a voluntary basis, a Land Rover based Fire Engine was supplied by the Northern Ireland Fire Service and the Fire Station is in one of the workshops at the Manor House.

## Churches

The Christian Church has been associated with Rathlin from the Sixth century onwards. In Church Quarter stands St Thomas' Church of Ireland on what was the earliest monastic site on the island. At the top of the brae stands the Roman Catholic Church which was built in the 1860s and dedicated to the worship of Almighty God by Most Reverend Patrick Dorrian, Bishop of Down and Connor, on 5th September, 1865. The Parish Priest was Rev. Michael McCartan. The Church and all its furniture were entirely free from debt on the day of its dedication. By the command of the Bishop the seats in the Church are common to all and cannot become the property of private individuals. Since that time, the Church has been renovated and improved several times. In 1930 the gallery was added. This work was carried out by Peter Dallat of Ballycastle. In the 1950s it was re-plastered by Kevin Black of Glacklugh.

The most recent and most extensive renovation was carried out in 1991 under the supervision of Fr Gerry MacAteer, since retired in 1999. All the plaster was stripped out back to the stonework, then two coats of bitumen based damp proofer was applied to the walls up to eaves height. The walls were then re-plastered. My own role in this was replacing some roof timbers which were found to be rotten. This was done from inside, without disturbing the roof slates. Later, I fitted new wood screens at the entrance and new doors and seating. The plastering was carried out by McVeighs of Ballycastle. Frank Darragh worked with myself and McVeighs throughout the renovation.

The present Catholic Church stands on the site of an earlier Church. This earlier Church had been a water mill and in 1817 was purchased from the Landlord for £48. It was extended and re-roofed and served as a Church until the present one was built. The side wall of this former Church can still be seen, acting as a retaining wall to the rear of the present Church. Prior to the establishment of this first Church, Mass had been said at various Mass Rocks around the island. Some of these are still known. There is one in Kilpatrick at Altbeg, where Fr MacAteer said a mass in July, 1998, the first since about 1815.

St. Thomas's Church was built about 1815 and stands on the site of an earlier Church built about 1722. It was in 1815 that the square tower was built. The graveyard at this Church has served all denominations on the island for several hundred years. The earliest gravestone marks the burial place of James Boyd, who died on 9th December, 1665. This burial is the first one marked, however, it is an indication that this graveyard had been in use from an earlier time, probably extending back to the time of the monastery in the Seventh century.

# Schools

The earliest mention of a school on Rathlin is in 1728, when a Daniel McNeile was schoolmaster. This was, of course, when the McDonalds of Antrim still owned the island. This schoolmaster had been procured by Bishop Hutchinson, C of I. The main purpose seems to have been to convert the children from the Irish language to English. This thinking was in line with the Penal laws when, among the many restrictions placed on the Irish people to do with Church worship and land tenure, it was also forbidden to speak Irish.

This school seems to have existed at least until 1795. After that time there was no regular school, apart from visiting teachers who came to the island during the summer time. These travelling or 'hedge' teachers do not appear to have pleased the landlord. He regarded them as unhelpful and political agents, out to create trouble. Of course they may have had a political agenda, as this was the time of considerable activity by all shades of opinion, which was organised by the Presbyterian United Irishmen, leading up to the Rebellion of 1798.

The next mention of regular schools comes in the Ordnance Survey Memoirs of 1830-35. The following schools are listed: Church Quarter, established 1824 as boys' school, 40 Catholics, 15 Protestants. School supported by the Kildare Place Society. The scholars pay 1 penny per week.

Demesne, established 1826 as girls' school, supported by the London Hibernian Society. Catholics 27, Protestants 3. Pupils pay 1 penny per week.

Cleggan, established 1827, supported by the London Hibernian Society. Pupils pay 1 penny per week. 25 girls, all Catholic.

Ballygill South, established 1835 as boys' school. Private school. Gaelic taught. Pupils pay 1 penny per week. 40 boys, all Catholic.

In addition to these four schools, there was another school held in a barn in Kinraver. This was independent, the master was Alexander Black. Pupils paid, 6 girls, 8 boys, all Catholic. There was a further school in Kinkeel, the mistress was Elizabeth Campbell, again held in an old barn, 9 boys and 9 girls. 13 Catholic and 5 Protestant. The total number of pupils recorded as attending was 182. The island population was over 1,000 in the 1820s and 30s. All these schools remained in use up until the early 1840s. With the arrival of the famine period, people left the island in large numbers, so that by 1861 the population was down to 453, by which time 4 of these schools had closed.

In 1875 the National School Board stated that the number of children attending did not warrant two schools and so the girls' school in Demesne was closed and the pupils started to attend the school in Church Quarter. This is the school which is still in use. There has been a school on this site for over 270 years. The present school was completely renovated in 1995, under the supervision of Fr G MacAteer. A small annex was built to the rear and the roof completely re-slated, as well as internal plastering and fittings. In this year, 1999, there are

Photograph at Rathlin School about 1930. I have not been able to identify the remaining pupils.
1. John McCurdy, Kinkeel; 2. Mick McQuilken, Ouig; 3. Seamus McCurdy, Cleggan; 4. Patsy McCurdy, brother of Seamus; 5. Dan McCurdy, Kinkeel; 6. John Cecil, Castle Quarter; 7. James McFaul, Glack an Tighe Mor; 8. Joe McCurdy, Post Office

Photograph 1930
1. Maggie Smyth, Park; 2. Kathleen McMullan, Ally; 3. Kate Maguire, Brockley; 4. Mary Maguire, Brockley; 5. Bridget McCurdy, Post Office; 6. Kathleen McPolin; 7. Miss McHenry, Teacher

**Rathlin Primary School Boys Class of 1957**
Front row (l to r): Jim McFaul, Robert McAuley, Peter McCurdy, Hugh
McQuilken, John Scanlon, Tommy O'Donnell, Anthony McCuaig, Alec Anderson
Middle row (l to r): Dominic McCurdy, Frank McCurdy, Maurice McCurdy,
Martin McCurdy, Noel McCurdy, Raymond Curry
Back row (l to r):Hugh O'Donnell, Neil McFaul, John Curry, Thomas Cecil,
James McAuley, Gerald McCurdy, Gerard McCurdy, Vincent Cecil

five pupils attending. This is the lowest figure in the history of the island schools.
When the children reach the age of eleven, they have to go to the mainland for
secondary education. Many go on to third level - very few return to live on the
island. Rathlin does not offer any employment, apart from a few tourist-related
summer jobs.

The past twenty years have seen a number of infrastructure improvements
on the island. These have brought the island almost up to mainland standards.
The first of these improvements was a mains water scheme for the dwellings in
the vicinity of the harbour. Whilst this is beneficial, it does not extend to the rest
of the island, where spring wells are the only source of water. There was
additionally a sewerage scheme to the same area.

### Electricity

The first major improvement was the installation of the mains electricity
scheme in 1992. This is generated on the island by a combination of wind-
powered turbines and diesel powered generators. The system was installed and
is maintained by Northern Ireland Electricity. Most of the capital cost was

provided by the European Commission and so on 16th October, 1992, the system was switched on by EC Commissioner, Mr Brian Millan, in the presence of three members of the European Parliament, Mr John Hume, Mr Ian Paisley and Mr John Nicholson, as well as Rathlin Development and Community Association Chairman, Mr Noel McCurdy and committee, NIE officials and all the islanders.

### The Children of Lir

The wind turbines on the Kilpatrick hill are named after the three sons of King Lir, Conn, Fiachra and Aedh. This is an ancient legend connected with Rathlin. This mains electricity has made a great difference to life on the island. Prior to this, each home had a diesel generator which was used only in the evenings to provide lights. If power was needed during the daytime, the generator had to be started first.

### Music, Song and Dance

Throughout the generations, Rathlin has had a strong tradition of song, music, dance and story telling. This tradition arose naturally from the Irish and Scots Gaelic origins of its people. The long winter nights gave ample opportunity to practice these skills. I can recall going visiting, as a child with my parents in the 1930s and 40s, to various houses during the winter. This visiting was known by the Gaelic word 'ceili'. "Going for a ceili", literally an evening visit. At that time the population was much larger than the present, around 250, and of course, there was no such thing as television.

Some houses had a radio, which worked off a battery or accumulator. This battery had to be charged up every few weeks, and so the radio was only used to listen to the news broadcasts, from either Radio Eireann or BBC. The only other modern gadget was a gramophone of the wind up type. We had one in our house and a small collection of the old 78 records. These were sent to us by my uncle and aunt who lived in Belfast. The records were usually of American dance bands of the day, singers such as Bing Crosby and Frank Sinatra and records of traditional Irish music and of John McCormack, the great Irish tenor. These records were very popular and I have seen them carried with the gramophone to various social functions on the island.

My father was a good singer in the Irish language, he also played the fiddle. I can recall him singing at various wedding receptions etc. There were a number of other good singers and musicians on the island, in fact nearly every home had someone who could sing or play an instrument. Many of the McCurdys could sing, also the Blacks. The Black family at Glacklugh, who were our nearest neighbours, were noted for music and song - every one of them could sing and play an instrument. Their modern day descendants are Mary and Frances Black, who are known internationally as singers of very considerable talent.

- 71 -

Another singer with Rathlin connections, and known on the world operatic stage, is Angela Feeney. Angela's people were from Cleggan and known as the John Roe McCurdys. There are still many good singers on Rathlin and they can be heard at Ceilis in the parish Hall or at parties. Unfortunately, only a few of the old traditional songs are now remembered.

The islanders were also great dancers and they still are to the present day. There are many traditional dances still danced on the island, such as The Lancers. This is an eight hand set. Also the six hand reel. Some other dances were The Pride of Erin Waltz, St Bernard Waltz, Hesitation Waltz, Military Two-step, Highland Schottische and the Versa Vienna, or as it is now know, Shoe the Donkey.

The Lancers consists of five parts and is fairly long, at least ten minutes. Over the years the tunes played for The Lancers have varied a good deal. Some I remember are The Saints, Red River Valley, Fare Thee Well Enniskillen and Coming Round the Mountain. There were also more traditional tunes, depending on the skill of the musician. The Lancers was always popular and still is now. Other dances such as the Haymakers Jig, Walls of Limerick, Siege of Ennis and Six hand Reel are still popular.

Social evenings in the Parish Hall were always important events and were fairly frequent, but less so nowadays. All of these dances and more would be danced in the course of the night. To give the dancers and musicians a break, various singers would be persuaded to give a song at intervals. Another break would be when tea and sandwiches and home-made cakes were served up to all, by a few of the ladies present. These evenings were very popular and were attended by all.

Before the Parish Hall was opened in 1914, various events, such as dances and plays were held in the Kelp Store and also in what is known as the Tithe Barn, next to the Manor House. Social evenings were also held in the Glebe Hall, which belonged to the Church of Ireland. Another winter pastime was card playing. This would go around the houses - usually Twenty-five was played. Prizes would be a goose or a hen. There were also whist drives organised in the Parish Hall.

Over the centuries various visitors to the island have mentioned hearing songs and stories in the Irish. One of these was a collector named Eamon McGregor. He collected stories from Daniel McCurdy of Kinraver and Archie Morrison of Brockley. These stories were first published in 1910 by M H Gill Ltd. in Dublin. There are two songs also written down, possibly by McGregor, but also by Sean Greene of Ballycastle, whose people were from Donegal.

"Mo Maire Og" was collected from Mrs Margaret McCurdy of Brockley, the second was "fear an Bata", and was collected from Mrs Katie Glass of Ouig. There is a third song "The Wedding of Donal and Maire". This was recorded a few years ago by a Donegal group "Altan". It had its origins in Rathlin and was

Johnny "John Roe" McCurdy

Mary "John Roe" McCurdy
nee Morrison
Mother of Daniel, John, Annie,
Isabella, Frances, Elizabeth

Frances "John Roe" McCurdy
Good Shepherd Nun in Ceylon for 60 years

**Annie and Isabella "John Roe" McCurdy about 1908
at their Milliners Shop, Newtownards Road, Belfast**

**Maggie, Mary Anne and Daniel "John Roe" McCurdy, Gortconny,
formerly Lathrach da Dhuibhean, Rathlin
"Lar-ta-Yiven", the old building of the dark glen**

**Photograph taken about 1920**
**Front: Augustine McCurdy, Garvagh; Loughie Black, Ballygill**
**Back: Mickey Joe Anderson, Glacanacre; Lady possibly Mattie Preston, related to**
**Mickey Joe; Paddy Black, brother of Loughie; Patrick Black (William), Ballygill**

**Photograph taken about 1920**
**James McCurdy, Elizabeth McCurdy, Mary Margaret McCurdy,**
**Joseph McCurdy (my grandfather) - all of Garvagh**

**Photograph taken about 1929**
Mary Margaret McCurdy, Garvagh; Paddy Black "Red", Ballygill;
Clare Anderson, Post Office; Tessie Black Glacklugh, later McCurdy;
Mickey Joe Anderson (at back); Augustine McCurdy (my father);
Kathleen McCurdy (my mother); Mary Anderson, later McCurdy, Post Office

**Mary Black in her shop, Rathlin about 1980**

taken to west Donegal by a stone mason from Rathlin. There is a song included in a book by Mrs Campbell which has the same title and may be the same song; the music given is a slow jig time. I include the words of these songs and a few others at the back of this book.

The Irish language of Rathlin had a good deal of Scots Gaelic intermixed. This was not surprising as many people on Rathlin had Scottish origins. This, of course, was not exclusive to Rathlin. The coastal areas, from the Antrim glens to west Donegal, had a similar ethnic and language mix. Nils M Holmer, a Swedish language specialist, came to Rathlin in August, September and October, 1937 and again in October, 1938. The purpose of this visit was to research and record what remained of the Irish on Rathlin. He received grant assistance from the Royal Irish Academy, Dublin. This research was published in 1939, by RIA, under the title of "The Irish Language in Rathlin Island."

During the first years of the 20th century serious attempts were made to restore the language in Rathlin. One of the most prominent people behind this movement was Francis Joseph Bigger, a well known solicitor in Belfast. Another was Roger Casement. The first Glens Feis was held in 1904 in Cushendall. Casement and Bigger hired a steamer for this event. Many people from Rathlin went on the steamer to the Feis and were brought home again the following day. It was at the Feis that Neil McCurdy "The Piper" won the piping competition. The prize was a set of pipes. These were the Scottish or 'marching' pipes. These pipes were in North Cleggan for many years, in the house of Patrick "John Pharaic" McCurdy, who was a relation of Neil "The Piper".

Kevin Black, of Glacklugh, told me that he was working in Carnlough as an apprentice plasterer in the 1920s. He asked Paddy if he would sell the pipes and Paddy said he would for 10/- (50p), so the next time Kevin came home he had saved up the 10/-. (It is worth noting here that wages for an apprentice at the time would have been 10/- per week.) Anyhow, Kevin bought the pipes and took them back to Carnlough. He was not allowed to play the pipes in the digs, so he had to play them out in the street. This did not please the residents of Carnlough, particularly some of the rebel tunes that Kevin knew. He was told that if he continued playing the pipes, he would get no more work in Carnlough. Kevin left Carnlough soon after and went to Dublin, where he continued his trade and music.

I remember visiting Kevin and his brother John in Dublin about 1948. They took me to a traditional music bar in Dublin, not too far from where Kevin lived. Kevin played the pipes that night. I have wondered since what happened to these historic and much travelled pipes. This Kevin Black, RIP, was of course the father of Mary and Frances Black.

There was a Priest in the island at the time, Fr Eddie McGowan. He was deeply involved in the Gaelic revival and wanted to have Irish taught in the school. This was opposed by the Landlord, who controlled the school at the time and also by Rev Kerr, Cof I Minister. The teacher of the time, Mrs Bridget Anderson, did not have Irish herself, so there was a problem. Fr McGowan brought in a Mr Tohill to teach Irish. Of course, he was not allowed to teach in the school, so he arranged night classes which were well attended. Most of the parents withdrew their children from school in protest at not being allowed to learn Irish at school. Mr Tohill was succeeded by Mr Boyle and he, in turn, by Miss Rose Doherty, a native speaker from Donegal. Fr McGowan ordered scrolls for the island boats, with names in Irish, from Stephen Clarke, who was a carpenter and furniture maker from Murlough and was, at the time, managing the Irish Home Industries Shop at Ann Street, Ballycastle. This shop finally closed in 1982 and will be remembered by many. Fr McGowan got permission from the Bishop to start building a new school where Irish would be taught. He did not expect funding to be a problem, as he expected that every Gaelic class in Ulster would contribute to the cost. He asked Francis Joseph Bigger for suggestions for an appropriate design for the new school. However, this project did not get started. Fr McGowan was transferred to a new parish and was replaced by Rev A McKinley in 1909, who was Parish Priest, as Rathlin had, once again, become an independent parish.

Fr McKinley was the first Catholic Manager of the school. His predecessor was Rev. Kerr. Matters settled down after this, parallel to this dispute, there had also been a long-standing argument over the state of the school premises. The Landlord had been offered a grant by the Education Board, as far back as 1896, to improve the school, but it had never happened. Finally, in 1912, the school was improved under Fr McKinley's supervision and, apart from painting, very little else was done to it until 1994, when it was completely renovated, including central heating and a new roof and small extension. This was carried out under the supervision of Fr MacAteer, recently retired Curate of Rathlin.

### St. Malachy's School of Irish

It was in 1908 that my father won a scholarship with the Gaelic League and attended Cloughaneely College in Donegal, where he attained the Gold Fainne. The Gaelic League continued to be involved in Rathlin and in 1914 St. Malachy's School of Irish was set up on the island. The founders and lecturers involved with this project read like a Who's Who of the Gaelic Revival. It is worth noting that many of these enthusiasts and scholars were Presbyterians.

In the report produced at the time, the management committee is listed as follows: President: Francis Joseph Bigger; Hon. Treasurers: Miss Gough, Coleraine, Miss Ide McNeill, Cushendun; Hon. Secretaries: Miss M Dobbs, Cushendall; James McFaul, Belfast; Assistant Secretary and Registrar: Michael McGuigan, Belfast. Professors: Roisin McCafferty, Michael McGuigan and Sean

Greene. All of these last three holding certificates from Cloughaneely College. The school was formally opened on Sunday, 5th July, 1914, the first term starting on the following day, Monday 6th July, and ending on Saturday, 29th August.

During the course various lectures were given by the following: Rev. A McKinley, PP of Rathlin, Mrs Alice Stopford Green, F J Bigger, Rev. Bro. Craven, Louis Walsh MA, James McFaul.

The report states that there were students from Dublin, Belfast, Dundalk, Omagh, Derry, Omeath and Ballycastle. Hours of classes were 10 am to 12 noon

**St. Malachy's School of Irish (Photograph courtesy of Mrs. Dora McCurdy)**

and 2 pm to 4 pm daily, Saturday 10 am to 12 noon. Tuition fee was 10/- for the whole term. Lodgings on the island were 10/- per week. Cheap train tickets from Belfast to Ballycastle were available. Boats to the island were the motor boat "Fainne Geal an Lae". This boat was presented to the island by the Gaelic League. There were other sailing and rowing boats available. Thirty one students were enrolled in the first term. Various ceilis, debates etc were organised. All of this took place in the newly-opened Parish Hall.

The summer school was repeated in 1915. Unfortunately, despite the enthusiasm of the founders, the language continued to decline, both in Ulster and Rathlin. There are no native speakers left on the island. However, as the old saying goes, "It's a long road that has no turning". The language is flourishing in Ulster now as never before, and we are in the process of establishing an Irish Class on Rathlin, using a high tech method, known as Video Conferencing.

Francis Joseph Bigger was well known to islanders, however, there were some individuals who thought that his influence was greater than anyone else,

**Gaelic Visitors leaving Rathlin August 16th 1908**
1. Stephen Clark, Ballycastle; 2. Joseph Anderson, Mullin Dreas, Rathlin;
3. John McCurdy, Castle Quarter, Rathlin; 4. James McFaul, Belfast;
5. Johnny McKinley, Rathlin; 6. Johnny Anderson, Rathlin
Note the Gaelic Banners on the boats. Photograph courtesy of Mrs Dora McCurdy

**Fainne Geal an Lae - Lying in Ushet Port, Rathlin**
This boat was steam driven and was presented to Rathlin by the Gaelic League.
She was eventually wrecked in a storm at Ushet Port.
Photograph courtesy Loughie McQuilkin

even the Clergy. I came across this story when researching Bigger's papers in Belfast.

There was an election in 1906 and one of the candidates in North Antrim was Rev W Moore from Kilrea. He wrote to F J Bigger, asking him to persuade the Rathlin Nationalist voters to abstain from voting. He said that there were 12 Unionist voters and 66 Nationalist. Of course, these votes were all men, as women did not have the vote at this time. He asked Bigger to meet them at Ballycastle pier and induce them not to vote for his opponent Glendinning. Bigger, of course, would not have anything to do with such a scheme. The islanders did go to Ballycastle to vote, unlike today where a polling booth is set up at the island school on Election Day.

### Kitchens and Fireplaces

The kitchen was the most important room in the house. The main fireplace was in the kitchen, usually on an internal wall, thus warming any adjoining room. The open fire was where all the cooking and baking was done. There was usually a crane built into the hob on one side of the fire. On this crane a pot or griddle was suspended over the fire by means of a short piece of chain and a crook. The crane could be swung out from the fire to lift a pot off or put one on.

The basic cooking utensils were the round bottomed pot, the oven pot, the griddle and the kettle. All these items were made from heavy iron, which, although heavy to handle, were excellent for cooking. They were designed to hang over the open fire. The round bottomed, three legged pot was used for many tasks - boiling potatoes, making porridge, making stew etc. The oven pot was flat bottomed, with a flat dished lid. It was used for baking a cake or making a roast. It was often set directly into the fire and hot coals built up around it and on the lid. The cakes or roast had a flavour which cannot be matched in today's modern high tech cookers. The next essential was the griddle, which was used for baking the traditional soda farls or potato bread, which are still available from the bakeries today. The fourth essential was the large iron kettle, which was kept on the hob, full of water, always near to boiling and, if it was needed for making tea, was set on the fire to boil up. There were a few other items which were used occasionally, such as the heavy iron frying pan and one or two iron saucepans.

The kitchen was usually the largest room in the house. It was all-purpose, meals were taken in it, people sat around the fire at night. The furniture consisted of a large kitchen table, a settle bed built against a wall (this was used as a seat or as a bed if needed), a few three-legged stools, maybe one or two high backed chairs. There would also be one or two benches or forms, which were brought into use if there was a crowd in for a party or card playing. Other standard items were a dresser, where all the crockery was kept, and a churn for making butter.

Sour cream for butter making was kept in a large earthenware crock on a small table in the corner. The heat of the kitchen turned the cream sour; this was essential as fresh cream would not churn. Churning with a hand staff required a good deal of energy and skill, especially in the winter, when the butter was slow to break. When this happened, the grains of butter were gradually gathered into one lump with the staff and then lifted out onto a flat board, where it was worked and beaten with butter spades and clean water to remove any remaining sour milk. Salt was then added and the butter shaped into blocks or prints. These prints were wooden moulds which would take half a pound and imprint a pattern such as wheat grains or a swan or various others. The sour milk or buttermilk was kept for baking, or it made a very refreshing drink.

**"The Garvagh Kitchen", 1930s**

### Treasure on Rathlin

On 16th June, 1931, Mr Bill Curry was repairing a fence at the cliffs on his land at Ballyconaghan, when he came across a hoard of coins which had been dug out and scattered by rabbits. The coins were eventually acquired by the then Ministry of Finance at Stormont, under the law of Treasure Trove. The coins dated from 1553 to 1641. This last date is very significant as it was the year of rebellion.

It was the following year, 1642, when the Campbells invaded the island and carried out the massacre, clearly the owner of the coins did not survive to recover his coins, quite a lot of money in those days, and not the sort of thing that would be easily forgotten. The list of coins is preserved at the Public Record Office in Belfast, and are as follows: Queen Mary I - 3 groats; Queen Elizabeth I - 33 shillings, 28 sixpences, 1 groat, 1 threepence; King James I - 1 half-crown, 16 English shillings, 2 Irish; shillings, 4 sixpences; King Charles I - 1 half-crown, 11 shillings

These coins were put on exhibit at Carrickfergus Castle, however, a few years ago enquiries were made as to their whereabouts and it seems that many of the coins have disappeared.

There have been one or two other small finds of coins, a few of Robert the Bruce and his son David were found at Bruce's Castle. Also some silver coins of Edward I, Edward II and Henry IV. These are all from the time of Robert the Bruce. No-one knows where these coins are now, possibly in a private collection.

### Some Notes on the name McCurdy

The name McCurdy, MAC UIREATRAIGH, phonetically MA-KYR-TAR-I, has been associated with Rathlin for many centuries. It has been mentioned in connection with Robert the Bruce, supporting his campaign in 1306. In the Hearth Money Rolls of 1669, there are two of the name in Rathlin and also a number on the mainland, in the Route and Culfeightrin. There is a tradition that the only survivor of the massacre carried out by the Earl of Essex in 1575 was a woman by the name of McCurdy.

The name has been translated as SEA-RULER. It has also been linked to the name MORIARTY. The spelling in Irish is almost identical, MUIRCHEARTAIGH. One researcher states that the name derives from CAIRBRE RIADA of the DAL RETI who went to the island of Bute in Scotland in the year 258 A.D. with his followers from the north Antrim territory of the Dal Reti. In a reference to the name in the "MacDonnells of Antrim" it is stated that Norse Chroniclers of 1156 and 1164 spelt the name of SOMERLED MAC GILABRIDGE (the overlord of Argyle) as SOWDRY MAC ILLURDY, which is one of the many spellings of the name. In Scotland the modern spelling is MC KIRDY. The variety of spellings of this name and most other Gaelic names arose through the attempts of officers or surveyors working for the Crown, writing down these names, as they heard them, phonetically. They had, in most cases, no knowledge of the Gaelic language, some managed to write down a version which preserved the original sound, but the majority were garbled translations to English or Lowland Scots.

In the year 1210, Jane Mac Donnell, great grand daughter of the aforementioned Somerled, was married to Alexander Stewart, the son and heir of Walter Stewart, the High Steward of Scotland. Through this marriage, Stewart gained control of much of Bute and Arran. At this time the Mac Reuda (McCurdy) were the principal possessors of Bute. As time passed by, the Stewarts sought to impose control over the whole island of Bute. By the year 1489 the McCurdys were forced to apply to King James IV of Scotland for a Crown Grant of their lands. A general charter was isued for the island of Bute. This document is in Latin and is deposited in the Register Office, Edinburgh. The spelling of the name is MAKUREDY, which is not too far from the Gaelic sound.

A number of American McCurdys claim descent from five brothers, Daniel, Petheric (Patrick), David , William and John, who, because of religious persecution, left Bute in an open boat in November, 1666. After a couple of days they landed on Rathlin, but apparently the following day they went on to Ballintoy, where they settled around "The Cairn". They must have been aware that Stewarts of Bute were already settled there and that there were McCurdys in the Route area, westwards towards the river Bann. The Stewarts were closely connected with the McDonnells of Antrim and acted as their land agents. They were able to provide their former neighbours on Bute, the McCurdys, with land holdings.

In 1989, there was a reunion of McKirdy/ McCurdys on the Isle of Bute, organised by Mr J McKirdy of Rothesay and Mr William McKirdy of Kelso. I attended this gathering, along with John and Dominic McCurdy of Rathlin and James McCurdy of Ballycastle. There were about 250 attended from around the world. It was a very enjoyable gathering. However, it has so far not been possible to repeat it.

The McCurdy name warrants further research as it is synonomous with the ancient kingdom of Dalriada and Rathlin.

## 53. mo Máire Óg.

### (A Rathlin Song.)

**I.**

D'ealuiġ m'aṫair 'r d'éag mo máṫair,
Ir ċan ḟeil mo ċáirdean le ḟáġail;
Aċt cad atá mé gan croḋ gan toiġ,
A beiṫ in dtóir ar Máire Óig.

*Luinneóg.*

Nó-ró-ró 'r gur tú mo rún,
Tug mé an gaol, 'r ċa b'aiṫreaċ liom,
Do'n niġin úd an ċúil dualaiġ ḋuinn,
Ir gur teiċ liom féin mo Máire Óg.

**II.**

Ċan ḟeil duine uasal ó nó barún,
Nó fear óg annr na feapann,
Naċ ḃḟeil dúil aca le bainir,
Aċ cuile fear, le Máire Óig.

**III.**

Ċan ḟeil duine 'ra ġleann úd ṫall—
Eadar bun 'r bárr a' ġleann'—
Naċ ḃḟeil ag bagairt ar mo ċeann
Ar ron a beiṫ in dtóir ar Máire Óig

**IV.**

Aċt ná cuireaḋ rin ort-ra brón
Faḋ ir béar mo ċuideaċt beo
Congḃóċaiḋ mire duit-re an lón,
Ir má ba rcóir ann ġeoḃaiḋ rin dram.

**Mo Maire Og**
**Collected by Eamon McGregor from**
**Mrs Margaret McCurdy, 1908, Brockley, Rathlin**

## 11.—FEAR A' BHÀTA—THE BOATMAN.

KEY A.—*Slowly, with feeling.*

```
{ :l, .,t, |d   :d .,s :m_r,d|t,   :r . :m .,l,|l,   :l, .,d :t, .,l,|l,,s, .- :m,
```

SEISD.  (Fhir a' bhàta, na hó-ro éi - le, Fhir a' bhàta, na hó-ro éi - le·
CHORUS.  O, my boatman, na hó-ro ai - la, O, my boatman, na hó-ro ai - la;

*Rall.*

```
{ :m, .,s, |l,   :l, .,l, :s, .,l,|d   :r .,m :l .,s |m   :r .,d :d .,t,|l,   :l,
```

(Fhir a' bhàta, na hó-ro éi - le, Mo shoraidh slàn dhuit's gach àit' an téid thu!
O my boatman, na hó-ro ai - la, May joy a-wait thee where'er thou sailest!!

'S tric mi sealltuinn o'n chnoc a's àirde,
Dh'fheuch am faic mi fear a' bhàta;
An tig thu 'n diugh, na 'n tig thu màireach
'S mar tig thu idir, gur truagh a tà mi.

Tha mo chridh'-sa briste, brùite;
'S tric na deòir a' ruidh o m' shùilean;
An tig thu nochd, na 'm bi mo dhùil rint,
Na 'n dùin mi 'n dorus, le osna thùrsaich?

'S tric mi foighneachd do luchd nam bàta,
Am fac iad thu, na 'm bheil thu sàbhailt;
Ach 's ann a tha gach aon diubh 'g ràitinn,
Gur gòrach mise ma thug mi gràdh dhuit.

Gheall mo leannan domh gùn do 'n t-sìoda,
Gheall e sud agus breacan rìomhach;
Fàinn' òir anns am faicinn 'iomhaigh;
Ach 's eagal leam gun dean e dìchuimhn'.

Ged a thu'irt iad gun robh thu aotrom,
Cha do lughdaich sud mo ghaol ort;
Bidh tu m' aisling anns an oidhche,
'Us anns a' mhadainn bidh mi 'gad fhoighneachd.

Thug mi gaol dhut, 's cha'n fhaod mi àicheadh;
Cha ghaol bliadhna, 's cha ghaol ràidhe;
Ach gaol a thòisich 'n uair bha mi m' phàisdein,
'S nach searg a chaoidh, gus an claoidh am bàs mi.

Tha mo chàirdean gu tric ag innseadh,
Gum feum mi d'aogas a leig' air dìchuimhn';
Ach tha 'n comhairle dhomh cho diamhain,
'S bhi tilleadh mara 's i tabhairt lìonaidh.

Bi'dh mi tuille tùrsach, déurach,
Mar eala bhàn 's i an déigh a réubadh;
Gulleag bàis aic' air lochan féurach,
'Us cach gu léir an déis a tréigeadh.

I climb the mountain and scan the ocean,
For thee, my boatman, with fond devotion:
When shall I see thee? to-day? to-morrow?
Oh! do not leave me in lonely sorrow.

Broken-hearted, I droop and languish,
And frequent tears show my bosom's anguish:
Shall I expect thee to-night to cheer me?
Or close the door, sighing, sad and weary?

From passing boatmen I'd fain discover
If they have heard of or seen my lover;
They never tell me—I'm only chided,
And told my heart has been sore misguided.

My lover promised to bring his lady
A silken gown and a tartan plaidie,
A ring of gold which would show his semblance;
But, ah! I fear me for his remembrance.

That thou'rt a rover my friends have told me,
But not the less to my heart I hold thee;
And every night in my dream I see thee,
And still at dawn will the vision flee me.

I may not hide it—my heart's devotion
Is not a season's brief emotion;
Thy love in childhood began to seize me,
And ne'er shall fade until death release me.

My friends oft tell me that I must sever
All thoughts of thee from my heart for ever;
Their words are idle—my passions, swelling,
Untamed as ocean, can brook no quelling.

My heart is weary with ceaseless wailing,
Like wounded swan when her strength is failing;
Her notes of anguish the lake awaken,
By all her comrades at last forsaken.

**Collected from Mrs. Katie Glass, Ouig**
**by Eamon McGregor 1908**

# Mount Grand

It was on Wednesday - Lammas Fair
We lassies went, with courage rare,
On motor boat to Rathlin Isle
To pass away a little while
The sea was calm, the sky was clear;
We started off without a fear.

But when we left our native shore,
Oh! How we longed for land once more;
But, favoured by a lovely day,
We landed safely in the Bay.
All sickness gone, and free from care,
Breathing now the Rachery air.

Seeing now we need not worry,
For on Mount Grand lives Mrs. Currie,
Who knows right well a trip at sea
Makes one long for a cup of tea.
The tea is made, the table spread
With jam and cake and barley bread.

We eat our fill and, glad to tell,
The Rachery tea has made us well
We scanned the Island o'er nad o'er,
And looked across from shore to shore;
But not a spot in all the land
Can equal or surpass Mount Grand.

The time has come to start for home;
The waves are high and topped with foam,
But Paddy knows the seaman's art:
While waves are high he will not start.
Over the waves a message flashed *-
"All well - shall come,"
If we can get a boat to cross.

*We thought it better not to hurry,*
*But stop the night with Mrs. Currie,*
*For, sure as we were born,*
*We would be sick in Slough na Moran.*


*Just one more sight - majestic, grand-*
*Of ocean, mountain, sea and strand*
*A sight of sights from where we stand;*
*And then farewell to you, Mount Grand.*


*\*The message over the waves was a telegraph*

*Courtesy of Loughie McCuaig,*
*author unknown*

# Rathlin Lights

O, many the day has come and gone,
A long and weary while;
Since last I saw the flashing
Of the Lights on Rathlin Isle;
As from the great Cunarder's deck,
Came swiftly into view;
The East Light and the West Light,
And the little Light on Rue.

Then my heart was sore and lonesome,
And my eyes with tears were full;
As I listened to the roaring
Of the waves upon the Bull;
I thought I smelt the heather
Where oft, a lad, I lay;
Keeping cows from out the barley
Through the long bright summer days.

When my head was full of fancies
And my heart was free from care;
Then it sang and fluttered gaily
As the skylark in the air;
But then the times got cruel bad,
And the farm we had was small;
With the old folk and the childer',
There was not room for all.

And so I left the Island,
And I sailed across the sea;
And the flashing lights of Rathlin
Were the last of home to me;
But, indeed, the luck was with me
In the city grim and cold;
As I toiled and saved the dollars
Like a miser saves his gold.

Now I've bought the little farm,
And I've got a motor boat;
And on the waters of the Moyle,
Be the proudest man afloat;
I am coming back to Antrim;
Never again to roam;
And the beckoning Lights of Rathlin
Shine out to guide me home.

Rachel W Hughes


Written early in the 20th Century, by Rachel Hughes

## The Rachray Man

Och, what was it got me that time
To promise I'd marry a Rachray man?
An' now he'll not listen to rason or rhyme,
He's strivin' to hurry me all that he can.
"Come on, an' ye be to come on!" says he,
"Ye're bound for the Island, to live wi' me."

See Rachray Island beyont in the Bay,
An' the dear knows what they be doin' out there
But fishin' and fightin' an' tearin' away,
An' who's to hinder, an' what do they care?
The goodness can tell what 'ud happen to me
When Rachray 'ud have me, anee, anee!

I might have took Pether from over the hill,
A dacent poacher, the kind of boy;
Could I keep the ould places about me still
I'd never set foot out o' sweet Ballyvoy.
My sorra on Rachray, the coul' sea-caves,
An' blackneck divers, an' weary ould waves!

I'll never win back now, what ever may fall,
So give me good luck, for ye'll see me no more;
Sure and Island man is the mischief an' all -
An' me that never was married before!
Oh think o' my fate when ye dance at the fair,
In Rachray there's no Christianity there.

# The Enchanted Island

To Rathlin's Isle I chanced to sail
When summer breezes softly blew,
And there I heard so sweet a tale
That oft' I wished it could be true.
They say at eve when rude winds sleep,
And hushed is every turbid swell
A mermaid rises from the deep
And sweetly tunes her magic shell.

And while she plays, rock dell and cave
In dying falls the sound retain,
As if some choral spirit gave
Their aid to swell her witching strain,
Then summoned by that dulcet note
Uprising to th' admiring view,
A fairy island seems to float
With tints of many a gorgeous hue.

And glittering fanes and lofty towers
All on this fairy isle are seen,
And waving trees and shady bowers
With more than mortal verdure green,
And as it moves the western sky
Glows with a thousand varying rays;
The calm sea tinged with each dye
Seems like a golden flood of blaze.

They also say if earth or stone
From verdant Erin's hallowed land
were on this majic island thrown,
For ever fixed it would there stand.
But when for this some little boat
In silence ventures from the shore
The mermaid sinks - hushed is the note;
The fairy isle is seen no more.

Published by Rev. Luke Connolly, Chaplain of Ballycastle Church 1810 - 1826.
Still sung on Rathlin.

# Pembroke Census Data for Rathlin Island Natives
### Compiled by John B. Craig

Key:    D = Dwelling No., in Order of Visitation
F = Family No., in Order of Visitation
PIW = Pembroke Iron Works
POB = Place of Birth
(Age) in Parentheses

**Census for 1850**

| | |
|---|---|
| D138/F138: | Black, Julius (28), Laborer |
| | Catherine (25) |
| D163/F169: | McCoy, John (25), Laborer |
| | Mary (22) |
| D164/F171: | Black, Alexander (31), Laborer |
| | Mary (28) |
| | Black, Archibald (24) |
| D171/F172: | Black, Archibald (27) |
| | Mary (28) |
| D227/F245: | McCurdy, Francis (25) |
| | Nancy (28) |
| | James (3) |
| | McCurdy, James (30) |
| | Bradley, James (22) |
| | Black, James (22) |
| D228/F241: | McCurdy, James (52) |
| | Nancy (48) |
| | John (15) |
| | Lauflin (14) |
| | Catherine (11) |
| | Margaret (8) |
| | Nancy (3) |
| D229/F249: | McFall, Neal (31) |
| | Margaret (28) |
| | Dan (8) |
| | Mary (5) |
| | McFall, Mary A. (50) |
| D238/F237: | Black, James (40) |
| D178/F179: | Morrison, James (24) Laborer |

**Census for 1860**

| | |
|---|---|
| D442/F 219: | John McFall (70), Farmer |
| | Elizabeth McFall (68) |
| | Ellen (28) |
| | Neale (24) |
| | James (16) |
| | Elizabeth (4/12) |
| D443/F220: | John McFall 2nd (60), Farmer |
| | Rose McFall (60) |
| | John McFall Jr. (30), Heaters Helper PIW |
| | Daniel McFall (28), Roller PIW |
| | James McFall (22), Screw Tender, PIW |
| D482/F263: | Laughlin Black (42), Shoe Maker |
| | Elizabeth Black (40) |
| | Joseph Morrison (24), Journeyman Shoemaker, POB Ireland |
| D516/F299: | Archibald Black (32), Lumberman |
| | Mary W. Black (30) |
| | Mary E. (2) |
| | Ann M. (7/12) |
| | Mary Weere (74) |
| | John Weere (74) |
| | Margaret Black (60) |
| | Archa (65) |
| D517/F300: | Archa McKinley (30), Lumberman |
| | Mary A. (28) |
| D518/F301: | Naile McCurdy (25), Iron Works |
| | Mary McCurdy (23) |
| | James Black (27), Roller, PIW |
| | John Black (25), Puddlers Helper, PIW |
| | John McCurdy (23), Roller, PIW |
| D519/F302: | John Anderson (44), Farm Laborer |
| | Christian Morrison (40), House Keeper |
| D521/F303: | John McCurdy 2nd (35), Laborer PIW |
| | Wife |
| D522/F305: | James Golding (28), Nail Packer PIW |
| | Margaret (Craig) Golding (27) |
| | John Crage (66), Laborer |
| | Ann Crage (62) |
| | Daniel Crage (40), Day Laborer |

| | |
|---|---|
| D526/F310: | Patrick McCurdy (60), Wheelwright |
| | Catherine McCurdy (56) |
| | James (33) |
| | Ann (23), Servant Girl |
| | Mary (20), Servant Girl |
| | Francis (19), Day Laborer |
| | Elizabeth (16) |
| | Catherine M. (13) |
| | Patrick (15), Day Laborer |
| D528/F312: | Patrick Wilkinson (32), Laborer |
| | Catherine Wilkinson (28) |
| | Daniel McKaye (80), Farmer |
| D529/F313: | Daniel P. McCurdy (30), Laborer |
| | Margaret A. McCurdy (33) |
| | Mary (11) POB Maine |
| | Ellen (11) " |
| | Margaret (9) " |
| | Lizza (7) " |
| | Catherine (6) " |
| | John C. (1) " |
| D530/F314: | Robert Anderson (34), Laborer PIW |
| | Mary Anderson (36) |
| | Peter (7) POB Maine |
| | Alexander (4) " |
| | Mary J. (1) " |
| F315: | Ann M. Larman (65) |
| | John (18), Laborer PIW |
| | Mary (14) |
| | Ann (16) Servant Girl |
| | Ester (12) |
| | Rose (10) |
| D531/F316: | Alexander McFall (37), Machinist |
| | Jane McFall (36) |
| F317: | Daniel Black (30) Heater in PIW |
| | Elizabeth Black (29) |
| D532/F318: | Patrick Black (40), Laborer PIW |
| | Archer Black (32) Day Laborer |
| | Betty Black (25) |
| D533/F319: | Neale Crage (27), Laborer PIW |
| | Catherine Crage (25) |
| D534/F320: | Daniel Wilkerson (55), Laborer |
| | Mary Wilkerson (55) |
| | Daniel (23) Laborer |
| | James (17), Laborer |
| | Michael (14) Laborer |
| D540/F329: | Neale Black (69) Wheelwrght |
| | Nancy Black (30) |
| | Rose (23) |
| | Laughlin (28), Heater PIW |
| | Neale (25), Heater PIW |
| D542/F331: | Michael Quinlin (40) Day Laborer PIW |
| | Catherine Quinlin (32) |
| D547/F336: | Alexander Larman (32), Heaters Helper PIW |
| | Chrisama Larman (32) |
| D548/F337: | Alexander Anderson (26) Day Laborer |
| | Sarah Anderson (25) |
| | Daniel Black (20) Roller Helper PIW |
| D553/F343: | Neale A. Black (25), Blacksmith |
| | Mary Black (60) |
| D534/F344: | John J. McCurday (68), Day Laborer |
| | Margaret McCurday (50) |
| | Mick (28) Day Laborer PIW |
| | Laughlin (26) Day Laborer PIW |
| | James (20), Day Laborer PIW |
| D560/F350: | John Black (30), Ship Carpenter |
| | Sophia Black (36) |
| D561/F351: | James Black (31) Day Laborer |
| | Mary Black (30) |
| | Neale McCurday (25)Puddler's Helper PIW |
| D562/F352: | James Anderson (30) Day Laborer |
| | Catherine Anderson (27) |
| D563/F353: | Rose Anderson, (65) |
| | Alex Anderson (24) Puddler's Helper PIW |
| D564/F354: | Alexander Morrison (45) Day Laborer |
| | Ann Morrison (35) |
| F355: | Alexander Crage (24) Day Laborer |
| D568/F360: | Neale McKay (30) Day Laborer |
| | Sarah McKay (30) |
| D587/F380: | William Anderson (36) Day Laborer |

Mary B. Anderson (29) POB Maine
D615/F410: John McKay (35) Day Laborer
Margaret McKay (40)
John (19) Pudlers Helper, PIW
Daniel (17) Roller PIW
Ann (15)
Neale (12)
James (7)
D616/F411: Frank McCurday (50) Day Laborer
Mary McCurdy (45)
Mary (23)
Frank (20) Day Laborer
James (12)

### Spouses of Rathlin Island Natives - 1860 Census
Michael Quinn and Elizabeth (BLACK) Quinn
Dennis Carney and Nancy (McCURDY) Carney
Frank Fahy and Mary (BLACK) Fahy
Cornelius Conley and Mary (BLACK) Conley
William Graham and Margaret (LAMOND) Graham

### Census for 1870
D45/F 47: McFaul, Neal (38), Farmer
Ellen (34), Kept House
Elizabeth (72)
D48/F48: McFaul, John (68) Farmer
James (32) PIW
Margaret (29) Kept House
D56/F60: Craig, Neale (33), Roller - PIW
Catherine (31), Kept House
D57/F61: McKay, Mary (43) Kept House
D118/F124: McCurdy, Francis (61) PIW
Mary (56) Kept House
James (20) Mariner
Catherine (18)
D175/F185: Black, Neal (68)
Neal W. (36) PIW
Ann (26) Kept House
D176/F186: Black, Laughlin (38) PIW
Mary (25) Kept House
Margaret (1/12) b. Ireland, May 1870?
D178/F196: Black Archibald (55) PIW
Mary (47) Kept House
Mary (74)
D180/F191: McCurdy, James (47) PIW
Margaret (44) Kept House
D183/F194: Wilkinson, Daniel (43) PIW
Ann (38) Kept House
D188/F199: Black, Archibald (62) PIW
Elizabeth (54)
Esther (100)
F200: Morrison, James (33) Shoe Maker
Margaret (24) Kept House
F201: McCurdy, John D. (30) PIW
Rose (30) Kept House
D189/F202: McCurdy, Patrick (74) Wheelwright
Catharine (65) Kept House
Mary (30)
Frank B. (27) PIW
D190/F203: McFaul, Alexander (44) Machinist
F204: McCurdy, Archibald (65) PIW
Esther (55) Kept House
F204: McKinley, Patrick (20) PIW
Mary (32) Born in Maine
John (48) PIW
D191/F205: Lamon, Alexander (40) PIW
Christy A. (37) Kept House
D192/F206: Black, Daniel A. (39) PIW
Elizabeth (42) Kept House
Patrick (44) PIW
Mary (70)
D193/F207: Bradley, John (34)
Nancy (40) Kept House
Sophia (65)
McKay, Neal 2nd (46) PIW
Catherine (36) Kept House
D195/F209: McFaul, John (39) PIW
Rosetta (29) Kept House
F210: McFaul, Daniel (37) PIW
Sarah (35) Kept House
Wilkinson, John (39)
D196/F217: Anderson, Catherine (37) Kept House
D197/F212: Anderson, Robert (45) PIW  .
Mary (47) Kept House
D199/F214: Morrison, Ann (51) Kept House
D204/F219: Christy ? (52)

D218/F220: McKay, John A. (53) PIW
Margaret (51) Kept House
D218/F222: McKay, Randall (72)
Mary (74)
D219/F223: Lamon, John (32) PIW
Rose (31) Kept House
F224: Lamon, Daniel (59) PIW
Mary (64) Kept House
Catherine (23)
D220/F225: Black, James (49) PIW
Mary (48) Kept House
D213/F224: McCurdy, Neal M. (51) PIW
D214/F230: Anderson, John (50) PIW
Christy (48) Kept House
D218/F235: Craig, Ann (77)
Daniel (50)
F236: McCurdy, Daniel B. (48) PIW
Margaret (45) Kept House
D221/F238: Morrison, Michael (64) Retired Ship's
Carpenter
Jane (49) Kept House
D222/F239: Black, Laughlin (59) Shoemaker
Elizabeth (60) (Sister?)
D227/F245: McCurdy, Joseph (35) PIW
D228/F247: Anderson, William (45) PIW
D229/F250: McCurdy, Daniel (35) PIW
Catharine (75)
D231/F252: McCurdy, John B. (74)
Margaret (68)
Laughlin (28) PIW
James (25) PIW
D232/F253: Black, Archibald B. (48) PIW
Sarah (40) Kept House
D242/F265: Black, John M. (47) PIW
Sophia (47) Kept House
D89/F104: Wilkins, Mary (64)
D201/F117: Black, Archer (42) Farmer
Elizabeth (40)
D211/F125: Lamon, Neil (36) Laborer
Nancy (33) Kept House

### Census for 1880
D33/F34: McFaul, Neil (47) Farmer
Helen (48) Kept House
Elizabeth (80)
D34/F35: McFaul, James (40)
Margaret (38)
D41/F42: Craig, Neil (46) PIW
Kate (44) Kept House
D308/F317: McFaul, Alexander (58)
Mary (55)
D314/F323: Morrison, Anne (60)
Alexander (28) PIW
Rose A. (23)
D315/F324: Golding, James (48) PIW Born in N.B.
Margaret (Craig) (48) Kept House
McCurdy, Mary (90) Aunt
D316/F328: Morrisson, Michael (70) Ret. Carpenter
Jane (60) Kept House
D319/F328: McCurdy, Neil H. (48) PIW
D320/F330: McCurdy, John D. (40) Farmer
Rose (41) Kept House
D322/F302: McKay, Neal (60) Laborer
Sarah (50) Kept House
D326/F333: McKiney, Archie (58) PIW
Catherine (40) Kept House
Peter (30) PIW
John (23) PIW
McKiney, John A. (60) (Brother) PIW
D326/F336: Bradley, John (46) PIW Rathlin??
Nancy (Black) (50)
Anderson, Michael (18) Adopted Son
D327/F337: Lamon, John (44) PIW
Rose (40)
D329/F339: Black, Neil (45) PIW
Ann (34) Kept House
D330/F340: McCurdy, James (63) Laborer
Margaret (54) Kept House
D331/F341: McKay, John (70) PIW
Maggie (63) Kept House
D333/F343: Anderson, Robert (75)
Mary (68) Kept House
D334/F344: Anderson, William (70)
Mary (50)

THE PEMMAQUON CALL

| D336/F346: | Anderson, Rose (90) |
| D337/F347: | McCurdy, Frank (40) PIW |
| | Jane (35) Kept House |
| D339/F349: | McCurdy, James A. (33) PIW |
| | Laughlin (44) (Brother) PIW |
| | Margaret (75) (Mother) |
| D340/F350: | Black, John M. (65) PIW |
| | Sophia (65) Kept House |
| D344/F354: | Wilkinson, Patrick (53) PIW |
| | Catherine (47) Kept House |
| | Neil A. (27) PIW |
| D344/F353: | McFaul, John (53) PIW |
| | Rose (40) Kept House |
| D348/F358: | Anderson, Catherine (47) Kept House |
| D349/F359: | McKay, Neil A. (59) Laborer |
| | Catherine (48) Kept House |
| D351/F361: | McCurdy, Catherine (54) Kept House |
| D352/F362: | Morrisson, James (41) Shoemaker |
| | Margaret (35) |
| | Black, Elizabeth (60) At House |
| D354/F364: | Black, Mary (35) Kept House |
| D355/F365: | Black, Daniel A. (46) PIW |
| | Elizabeth (50) Kept House |
| | Black, Mary (84) Mother |

| D363/F373: | McCurdy, Frank (77) Laborer - Retired |
| | Mary (65) Kept House |
| | Craig, Daniel (50) PIW (Boarder) |
| D428/F439: | Black, James (58) Farmer |
| | Mary (45) Kept House |

**Census for 1900**

| D310/F323: | Morrison, James (65) Shoemaker |
| | Margaret (56) |
| | Black, Elizabeth (83), Aunt |
| D313/F324: | McFaul, John (73) |
| | Rose (59) |
| D319/F341: | McFaul, Alec (76) Capitalist. Arrived |
| | 1847 - 53 years in US |
| D323/F347: | Anderson, Mary (73), Arrived 1848 - 52 |
| | years in US) |
| D132/F134: | Lamond, Neal (66) |
| | Nancy (64) |
| D174/F179: | Golding, James (57) Born in Canada |
| | Elizabeth (Craig) (53) Rathlin Island, |
| | Ireland |

**Census for 1920**

| D197/F203: | Morrison, Margaret (74), Arrived 1861, |
| | Citizenship 1868 |
| | Mary (51) Daughter |

SOURCE: US Census Data for Maine, Washington County, for the years 1850-1920. (1890 unavailable). Family Histor
Center Numbers: 443509, 443510, 0803455, 010235, 1254489, 1254490, 1240601, 1374559, 1820649, 182065

**Pembroke Ironworks, Maine, USA.
Many Rathlin emigrants worked here.**

| Name | Residence | Court | Vol-page | Birthplace | Birthdate | Naturalization Date | Date of Entry | Port of Entry | Witnesses |
|---|---|---|---|---|---|---|---|---|---|
| Arthur McCurdy | 11 Woodbury St Beverly, Mass | USDC Salem Ma. | 2-333 | Ireland | Feb 6, 1854 | Nov 3, 1891 | | | |
| Brenton H. McCurdy | 2 James St. Boston, Mass | USDC Boston | 133-86 | Nova Scotia | July 17, 1860 | Nov 12, 1885 | | | |
| Daniel McCurdy | Boston Mass | Boston Municipal Ct | 1836 24-1388 | Great Britain | Sept 8, 1812 | Nov 7, 1836 | | | |
| Daniel McCurdy | Braintree Mass | USCC Boston | 35-137 | Nova Scotia | Nov 9, 1833 | Oct 30, 1868 | | | |
| Daniel McCurdy | Lubec, Maine | Washington Co SJ-Machias | 1A-251 | Ireland | - | Oct 10, 1860 | 1854 | | J.C. Talbot Jr. |
| Daniel McCurdy | Perry, Maine | Washington Co SJ- Machias | 1A-339 | Ireland | | Oct 3, 1865 | 1857 | | |
| David L. McCurdy | Lubec, Maine | Washington Co SJ - Machias | 1A-249 | Ireland | | Oct 1860 | 1854 | | J.C. Talbot Jr. |
| Edgar Henry McCurdy | 109 Hollingsworth, Lynn Mass | Lynn Mass Police Ct | 1885-1906 2-3217 | Great Britain | May 29, 1872 | June 6, 1906 | | | |
| Francis McCurdy | Pembroke, Maine | USDC Portland Me | 4-325 | Co. Antrim Ireland | 1837 | June 6, 1860 | Aug 1, 1853 | Eastport Me | Neil McCurdy - Pembroke, Daniel McFall Pembroke |
| Francis McCurdy Jr. | Pembroke, Maine | Penobscot SJ Bangor, Me | 4-336 | Ireland | | Sept 4, 1860 | 1850 | | Wm. E. Hewes |
| George Frederick McCurdy | 161 Brampton Way, Savin Hill, Boston | USCC Boston | 379-141 | New Brunswick | June 6, 1870 | Oct 10, 1900 | | | |
| Hayes Warren McCurdy | Roxbury, Mass | USDC Boston | 1-200 | Great Britain | May 13, 1825 | Apr 9, 1847 | | | |
| Henry McCurdy | Boston, Mass | USCC Boston | 81-18 | Nova Scotia | Oct 6, 1837 | Sept 28, 1874 | | | |

| Name | Residence | Court | Vol-page | Birthplace | Birthdate | Naturalization Date | Date of Entry | Port of Entry | Witnesses |
|---|---|---|---|---|---|---|---|---|---|
| John McCurdy | Lubec, Maine | Washington Co S.J. Machias | 1-127 | Ireland | Aug 1.1833 | Oct 1860 | July 4, 1851 | Pembroke Maine | |
| John McCurdy | Pembroke, Me. | SJ - Machias | 1A-55 | Ireland | | | 1849 | | |
| John McCurdy | Pembroke Me | Washington Co SJ- Machias | 1A-353 | Ireland | | | 1847 | | |
| John McCurdy | Pembroke Me | Washington Co SJ - Machias | 1-28 | Co. Antrim Ireland | Mar 17,1832 | Oct 7,1856 | June 1846 | East Port Maine | |
| John McCurdy | Perry, Maine | USDE-Portland | 4-331 | Co.Antrim Ireland | 1830 | Sept 6 1860 | 1852 | East Port Maine | |
| John McCurdy | Randolph, Me | Kennebec Co.Sup Ct-Augusta, Me | 2-104 | Gt. Britain & Ireland | | Sept 7, 1894 | | | A.B.Connor E.E. Norton |
| John McCurdy | So.Scituate,Mass | USDC Boston | 38-313 | Ireland | Mar 17, 1812 | June 17, 1861 | | | |
| John B.McCurdy | Pembroke, Me | USDC Portland | 3-189 | Co.Antrim Ireland | Apr 1, 1836 | Aug 31,1858 | Apr 1, 1853 | Eastport Maine | Laughlin McCurdy Pembroke Joseph McCurdy Pembroke |
| John E.McCurdy | 223 Cross St Malden, Mass | USDC Boston | 181-18 | New Brunswick | June 12,1858 | Oct 25,1892 | | | |
| Joseph McCurdy | Lubec,Maine | USDC Portland | 3-191 | Co.Antrim Ireland | May 20, 1834 | Aug 31, 1858 | Oct 1848 | Eastport Maine | George Ramsdell - Lubec Joseph Lamson-Lube |
| Laughlin McCurdy | Hopkinton, Mass | USDC Boston | 19-307 | Ireland | Feb 12,1804 | July 5,1856 | | | |

| Name | Residence | Court | Vol-page | Birthplace | Birthdate | Neutral-ization Date | Date of Entry | Port of Entry | Witnesses |
|------|-----------|-------|----------|------------|-----------|----------------------|---------------|---------------|-----------|
| Laughlin McCurdy | Lubec, Maine | USDC Portland | 3-193 | Co.Antrim Ireland | Mar.22,1836 | Aug31, 1858 | July 1847 | Eastport Maine | George Ramsdell-Lubec Joseph McCurdy-Lubec |
| Laughlin McCurdy 2nd | Lubec, Maine | USDC Portland | 3-195 | Co.Antrim Ireland | Dec 31,1828 | Aug 31,1858 | July 13,1849 | Boston Mass | George Ramsdell-Lubec Joseph Lamson-Lubec |
| Michael McCurdy | Calais, Maine | Washington Co SJ-Machias | 8-121 | St.David, Charlotte Co. New Brunswick | Apr.30, 1820 | July 1844 | 1822 | Robbinston Maine | |
| Neal McCurdy | Lubec, Maine | Washington Co SJ-Machias | 1A-77 | Ireland | | Apr 24, 1856 | 1854 | | |
| Neil McCurdy | Pembroke, Maine | USDC Portland | 4-333 | Co.Antrim Ireland | 1820 | Sept 16, 1860 | Aug 15, 1849 | Boston Mass | George Small - Pembroke, John McFaul, Pembroke |
| Patrick McCurdy | Arlington Vt | Bennington Vt Municipal Ct | 4-123 | Quebec Province | 1859 | Sept 1, 1894 | | | JC Farnum-Bennington, G.H. Grant, Bennington |
| Peter McCurdy | Boston, Mass | USDC Boston | B2-405 | Ireland | Mar 15, 1804 | Sept 20, 1839 | | | |
| Alexander McCurdy | 18 Dana St. Boston, Mass | USDC Boston | 219-21 | Nova Scotia | Apr 28,1867 | Sept 17, 1896 | | | |
| Alexander McCurdy | Gloucester, Mass | USCC Boston | 71-51 | New Brunswick | Jan 5, 1844 | Jan 8, 1873 | | | |
| Alexander McCurdy | Lubec, Maine | Washington Co SJ-Machias | | Ireland | | Apr 24, 1856 | | | |
| Alexander McCurdy | Manchester, Vt | Bennington Vt Municipal Ct | 4-53 | Quebec Province | 1855 | Aug 29, 1888 | | | |

| Name | Residence | Court | Vol-page | Birthplace | Birthdate | Natural-ization Date | Date of Entry | Port of Entry | Witnesses |
|---|---|---|---|---|---|---|---|---|---|
| Isaac McCurdy | 13 Grenville Boston, Mass | USCC Boston | 188-166 | | Sept26, 1862 | Oct 6, 1888 | | | |
| James McKirdy | Boston | Suffolk Co. Superior Criminal Ct, Boston | 5-229 | Great Britain | Aug 20, 1870 | July 8, 1864 | | | |
| James McCurdy | Pembroke Maine | Bangor, Me | 4-341 | Ireland | Of Age 25yrs | Sept 4, 1860 | 1853 | | Wm. E. Hewes |
| James T.McCurdy | Pembroke, Maine | Penobscot Co SJ Bangor, Me | 4-346 | Ireland | Of Age 29yrs | Sept 4, 1860 | 1849 | | |
| John McCurdy | Charlestown, Mass | USCC Boston | 4-737 | Ireland | June 12,1814 | Jan 15, 1853 | | | |
| John McCurdy | Charlestown, Mass | USCC Boston | 13-325 | Ireland | 1817 | Nov 2, 1860 | | | |
| John McCurdy | Hopkinton, Mass | USDC Boston | 20-1 | Ireland | May 21, 1827 | July 5, 1856 | | | |
| John McCurdy | Lubec, Maine | Washington Co SJ - Machias | 1-34 | New Brunswick | May 22, 1831 | Oct 7, 1856 | 1844 | Lubec Me | |